Death in the Queen City
Clara Ford on Trial, 1895

PATRICK BRODE

NATURAL HERITAGE BOOKS
TORONTO

Published by Natural Heritage / Natural History Inc.
P.O. Box 95, Station O, Toronto, Ontario M4A 2M8
www.naturalheritagebooks.com

Library and Archives Canada Cataloguing in Publication

Brode, Patrick, 1950-
        Death in the Queen City : Clara Ford on trial, 1895 / Patrick Brode.

Includes bibliographical references and index.
ISBN 1-897045-00-X

        1. Ford, Clara — Trials, litigation, etc. 2. Westwood, Frank.
3. Trials (Murder)— Ontario — Toronto. 4. Murder — Ontario — Toronto.
5. Toronto (Ont.)— Social life and customs —19th century. I. Title.

HV6535.C33T67 2005a   345.71'02523'09713541   C2005-903207-3

Front cover: top, newspaper sketches (l-r): Clara Ford, *News*, Nov. 28, 1894; Frank Westwood, *News*, Oct. 10, 1894; Coroner R.B. Orr, *News*, Oct. 16, 1894; bottom: York Street, looking north, 1856, *courtesy of the City of Toronto Archives, Fonds 1498, Item 16.* Back cover: left, Ebenezer Forsyth Blackie Johnston; right, Crown prosecutor Britton Bath Osler. *Photos courtesy of the Law Society Archives.*

Cover and text design by Sari Naworynski
Edited by Jane Gibson
Printed and bound in Canada by Hignell Book Printing of Winnipeg

Natural Heritage / Natural History Inc. acknowledges the financial support of the Canada Council for the Arts and the Ontario Arts Council for our publishing program. We acknowledge the support of the Government of Ontario through the Ontario Media Development Corporation's Ontario Book Initiative. We also acknowledge the financial support of the Government of Canada through the Book Publishing Industry Development Program (BPIDP) and the Association for the Export of Canadian Books.

TABLE OF CONTENTS

Acknowledgements   i

Introduction   ii

CHAPTER ONE	1	"Mother I Am Shot"
CHAPTER TWO	6	Inquest
CHAPTER THREE	16	Queen City
CHAPTER FOUR	24	"You Know My Color"
CHAPTER FIVE	34	A Complete Solution
CHAPTER SIX	44	Clara
CHAPTER SEVEN	62	The Sweatbox
CHAPTER EIGHT	75	Revelations of an Improper Sort
CHAPTER NINE	87	The Crown's Case
CHAPTER TEN	96	Confession
CHAPTER ELEVEN	106	Ribbons and Bullets
CHAPTER TWELVE	115	Clara's Version
CHAPTER THIRTEEN	126	Final Battle
CHAPTER FOURTEEN	139	Cheers In Court
CHAPTER FIFTEEN	148	Triumph

Notes   160

Bibliography   173

Index   177

About the Author   184

ACKNOWLEDGEMENTS

In the preparation of this study, I have been greatly assisted by Peter Oliver, the editor-in-chief of the Osgoode Society for Canadian Legal History, Susan Lewthwaite of the Law Society Archives, Carl Thorpe of the Multicultural History Society of Ontario, Victoria Gill of the Toronto Public Library, and especially by Stephen Otto, Janet and Angela Brown, Philippa Elmhirst, Vivian Robinson and by Norina D'Agostini of the Toronto Police Museum.

INTRODUCTION

It is one of the great joys of history that it enables us to experience a world very different from our own. While the trial of Clara Ford in 1895 is not that far removed from us in time, the Toronto of that era almost seems to be a foreign land. In manners and morals, Victorian Toronto was populated by a citizenry who had a view of right and wrong very different from our own. Not only has the face of the city greatly changed, but also attitudes towards sex, dress and those who did not "fit in" are a world apart from the commonly held views of a century ago.

The central character of this incident, Clara Ford, was a remarkable person for her or any time. She was Black at a time when people of African ancestry were considered exotic and occasionally unwelcome members of society. In both dress and mannerisms she refused to conform to what her community considered proper forms of feminine behaviour. Clara lived in a time when women were regarded as pure and simple creatures, and it was simply inconceivable for Toronto gentlemen to believe (as the prosecution would urge them to believe) that such an angelic creature as a woman could stalk and kill a man. Clara's irritating refusal to conform to expected patterns of behaviour makes her seem in some ways a more contemporary figure than that well-educated, but conventional, group of men who decided her fate.

CHAPTER ONE

"Mother, I Am Shot"

Just before 11 p.m., eighteen-year-old Frank Westwood answered the pull-bell at the door of his father's stately mansion in Toronto's fashionable Parkdale neighbourhood. So far, this Saturday, October 6, 1894, had been uneventful. Young Frank had been out on the town with a trio of pals and had returned about an hour earlier. For about an hour he had sat in the parlour of their house, "Lakeside Hall" as it was grandly known, looking out at the waters of Lake Ontario and chatting with his mother. These late-night chats were not unusual, for Frank was especially close to Clara Westwood and tended to confide in her. By about 10:30 they both went upstairs and Frank was preparing to go to bed when he heard a peculiar late night call. Going downstairs, he lit the gas jet in the hallway to shed some light and released the safety latch to open the front door that faced onto Jameson Avenue. Suddenly, there was a flash and the loud report of a revolver. A bullet struck Frank on the right side, just below the ribs

Sketch of how the shooting occurred, as taken from the description given by Frank Westwood, Toronto News, *Oct. 8, 1894.*

and he collapsed onto the carpet of the hallway crying out, "Mother, I am shot."[1]

Mrs. Westwood ran downstairs and called out to her husband Benjamin to come with his revolver as there were burglars in the house. The first thing Frank said to her was, "I opened the door and a man shot me." She asked him why he had not left the chain on the door, but he only turned his head away and pleaded, "Mother, don't scold me." Leaving her stricken son for a moment, Clara telephoned for a doctor. When she returned to the hallway, she found that Frank had stumbled upstairs to the room he shared with his younger brother Willie. Willie had been asleep when Frank, his vest now

Lakeside Hall, the Westwood residence on Jameson Avenue in Parkdale, Toronto News, *Oct. 8, 1894.*

awash in blood, almost collapsed into his arms. Mrs. Westwood, Willie and a maid helped hoist the injured youth onto a bed until medical help could arrive.

Meanwhile, Benjamin Westwood had gone outside but was unable to see anything. He fired his gun once to see if he could flush out the attacker, or if there were a number of burglars, to let them know that he was armed.

There was nothing there.

The entire incident, the call at the door and the firing of the shot had only taken a few seconds. Westwood strained his eyes up and down Jameson Avenue to try to see who had destroyed his family's tranquility that evening. But there was no one there. The only remnant of the incident was the boy upstairs with the hideous wound in his abdomen.

About fifteen minutes after the shooting, three doctors, Adam Lynd, Hart and Sparrow had rushed to Lakeside Hall and, in about the same time, constables from No. 6 Police Station had arrived. Although he was seriously hurt, Frank was able to talk and give the police a limited description of the attacker. He appeared to be of medium height, had a moustache and was wearing dark clothes and a fedora. Frank had never seen him before. The following Sunday morning, the police began to comb the grounds and the area around Jameson Avenue looking for clues. Frank's wound became increasingly painful and opiates were administered to relieve him. That morning, Sunday services across Toronto were sombre as the sad news filtered across the city. At the Westwood's church, Parkdale Methodist, the Rev. E.F. Scott pronounced that mysterious calamities sometimes visited households, but in the great hereafter all mysteries would be resolved.

It was readily apparent to the doctors that the trauma was fatal. On Monday the surgeons probed the wound and found that too many organs had been damaged to offer any prospect of survival. Frank had been an avid boater and outdoorsman who had spent much of his young life on the waters of Lake Ontario. In the ensuing days he asked his friends to come for a final visit. To one he gave his canoe, to another his share in a boat. All this time he chatted away amiably but occasionally lapsed into depression and could not speak.

On Monday Crown attorney James Walker Curry and the Chief of Detectives, William Stark, came to the house to record a final deposition. However, the doctors advised against it so long as he had a "fighting chance for life." Besides, the statement would only have legal effect if the victim was aware that death was upon him. In the ordinary course, only verbal testimony is accepted by the Courts. One exception to this rule is a statement made by a witness who knows that death is near and his testimony would otherwise be lost forever. By Tuesday it was clear that young Frank's life was ebbing away and Curry, this time assisted by a Toronto detective Charles Slemin, came to Frank's room to take down an *ante-mortem* statement that could be used at a future criminal trial. Undoubtedly Frank was aware of the purpose of their visit and was resolved to help as best he could. His mind was clear enough to enable him to make a statement that, for the moment, was to be kept secret.

In the meantime, the city was alive with rumours. "There is a girl in it"[2] was the most popular one and rested on the notion that a jealous rivalry must have motivated the killing. If he had stolen the affections of another man's woman this might explain the attack. Or was it a matter of honour? Had he disgraced a young woman to the extent that her family sought revenge? "The belief that there must be a woman at the bottom of it all has been embraced by many," wrote the Toronto *Mail*. In a candid interview, Chief of Detectives Stark commented that, "My own opinion is that there is a woman somewhere in the case," and, as Frank was largely unknown outside his own intimate circle, it was unlikely to be an act of public displeasure, "but under the present circumstances it looks like a case of revenge." The press agreed that this was the juiciest motive, for the *World* stuck by the theory that "the shooting was the outcome of the entanglement of the victim with a woman, that it was for her sake that the crime was committed." For the moment, the two detectives assigned to the case, George Porter and Charles Slemin, concentrated on the victim's immediate family and friends to try and find out who may have wanted revenge. They dug into Frank Westwood's likes and dislikes, his habits and movements to, at the very least, understand the victim in the hopes that it would lead to the criminal. Both detectives were aware of the importance of the case for they operated "with the knowledge that many eyes are watching them."

Despite the seeming dearth of information, the Toronto police seemed most optimistic, and it was reported, "the detectives profess now to see light through the darkness, and express the utmost confidence that within 48 hours they will have become possessed of all the facts of the case and have the perpetrator of the crime in custody."[3] As in so many cases of hubris, none of these predictions came to pass.

CHAPTER TWO

Inquest

On Wednesday morning, as the many church bells of Toronto began to toll, Frank Westwood died in his mother's arms. He died in his own bedroom overlooking the waters of Lake Ontario where he had spent so many hours of his short life. No one among his family and friends had any idea who would take the life of such a pleasant young man. To all, including the Toronto police, his death was a peculiar and stubborn mystery.

Frank's coffin was placed in the drawing room of Lakeside Hall surrounded by flowers including one in the shape of an anchor from his sailing companions.[1] The wreath bore the simple inscription "Comrade." The Rev. E.F. Scott delivered the funeral service and announced to the crowd (which spilled out of the house and down the street) that the young man had accepted Christ as his Saviour and had urged his friends to do the same. Such a late conversion seemed a trifle odd in an adolescent whose father was a pillar of the

Parkdale was besieged by newspaper reporters. These headlines are from the Toronto News, Oct. 8, 1894.

WHO SHOT WESTWOOD?

A Young Man, Eighteen Years of Age, Shot Down at His Father's Door.

PARKDALE IS AGITATED BY A SENSATIONAL MYSTERY.

Frank B. Westwood Lying Unconscious and at the Point of Death With a Bullet in His Body.

Methodist church. Then the Reverend spoke of the mysterious nature of the murder and surprisingly added a few comments on the character of the deceased "of the black and unmanly aspersions which had been cast upon the characters of many innocent and respectable people." Just who was Frank B. Westwood?

In theory, the answers were to come from the ensuing coroner's inquest.[2] However, the process began on an inauspicious note when the chief coroner mistakenly called for an inquest on Monday when Frank was still alive. The warrant was held and not issued until after the victim's death on Wednesday. Only then were the members of the coroner's jury sworn in and permitted to troop through the Westwood home to view the body.

The inquest, one of the oldest institutions of English law, had been devised in medieval times to enable the King to inquire into matters such as the loss of ships, treasure or the unexplained death of a taxpayer – all matters which affected the Royal purse. The coroner's jury survived into modern times as one of the few administrative juries to endure, but now its focus had shifted from lost revenues to the circumstances of a citizen's death. Still, in method it was more of a public scavenger hunt instead of a systematic investigation and it was usually of little use in resolving problems.

A sketch of Frank B. Westwood as shown in the Toronto News, *Oct. 10, 1894.*

At 8 p.m. on the evening of Friday, October 12, only two hours after Frank Westwood's rosewood casket was lowered into the grave at Mount Pleasant Cemetery, Coroner R.B. Orr called the formal inquest into his death to order. So sensational was the case that the old Parkdale town hall was crammed with the curious. Latecomers struggled to get in as a police cordon tried to keep some order. Crown attorney Hartley H. Dewart conducted the proceedings and began with the testimony of Benjamin Westwood. There was little that he could add to what was already known. His son had described the assailant as a moustached man of medium build and wearing dark clothes, but had not recognized him. The only suspicious incident of any conceivable relevance that Mr. Westwood could recall concerned a recent confrontation with a group of stonehookers.[3] These were the men who sailed offshore and levered slabs of limestone from the bottom of Lake Ontario for use in basement construction. Stonehooking was a hard, low-paying job and the men attracted to it were generally not well thought of in the community. Benjamin Westwood recalled an incident that past summer when some stonehookers had tried to break into their boathouse and he had fired warning shots to drive them off. Perhaps they had returned and sought revenge. In fact, there were some stonehookers just offshore

Benjamin Westwood at the inquest, Toronto News, Oct. 16, 1894.

at the time and one of them, Albert Peer, swore that he had heard the fatal shot.[4] He recalled that some men had paddled by in a canoe and warned the stonehookers not to go ashore "as they would get some lead in them." Despite these suspicions, there was no direct evidence against any of them.

The Crown attorney next called the pathologist, Dr. John Caven. Caven's autopsy had confirmed that the trajectory of the shot could only have come from a person standing directly in front of Frank. However, the shot was not so close as to leave powder burns on the clothes. Dr. Caven produced a little round pill box which contained the fatal .38 calibre bullet. The family physician, Dr. Lynd had assisted with the autopsy, and added that shortly after the shooting he had given Frank a sedative and probed for the bullet. At this time, Dr. Lynd had questioned him about the shooting and, curiously enough, "his first impression was that Frank was concealing something,"[5] but he later accepted Frank's story that he did not know the assailant. It was suggested early on that perhaps

Frank was not the target at all as the *World* speculated, "The assassin intended the shot for Mr. Westwood Sr. and in the uncertain light mistook the son for the father." An affronted Benjamin Westwood told reporters that he did not think he had any enemy who wished to kill him.

Subsequent witnesses seemed promising but offered little. The investigators had high hopes for the testimony of Mrs. Ellen Card who lived just down from the Westwoods on Jameson Avenue. She had spent the evening at the Grand Opera with her children and after the performance had taken the King Street streetcar home. She noticed a man in a light overcoat get off at Jameson but lost him in the crowd. As she walked towards the lake, she saw a man pause outside the Westwood house and then rush in. Samuel Sherwood, the conductor on the King Street run, testified that he had left Yonge and King streets at 11:06 p.m. and took about 18 minutes to get to Jameson Avenue. It was a busy evening and he had no idea who was on his car. However, as promising as Mrs. Card's testimony had seemed, the performance she had attended was not over until eleven that night and she could not have returned home until nearly 11:30, or about a half hour after the shooting. The man she had seen entering the Westwood property was almost certainly Dr. Lynd.

King Street on Saturday night was full of life, a vibrant thoroughfare where theatre-goers, pub-crawlers, the well-to-do and prostitutes all crossed paths. The Crown called a number of persons who were on King Street that night, but no one had heard anything out of the ordinary. The Westwood's maid, Bessie Stephen, was examined on any aspect of trouble or recrimination in the household, but she replied that they all seemed to be on the best of terms. Finally, Dewart called a neighbour, Henry Hornberry, who on the Monday after the shooting, took it upon himself to do some amateur sleuthing.[6] Underneath a tree he had discovered some twenty slips of paper that had once formed a single sheet. Hornberry pieced them together. The writing appeared to be in a lady's hand and read, "You said you would. If you do not, I will." What, if anything these words meant, no one knew. The inquest was clearly getting nowhere and, in frustration, Dewart tossed the paper fragments on the counsel table and requested an adjournment.

Hornberry, the amateur detective, had achieved minor celebrity status and, in interviews with reporters from both the *Mail* and the *Empire*, he described his find and developed his theory that a woman wearing men's clothing must have committed the murder. "You can say that my theory is that a woman did the shooting," Hornberry pronounced. He continued, "She was not the party who sought revenge, but was the hired assassin of the vengeance seeker." The police dismissed this as just one of the many crank stories that had come their way in recent days.

While Hornberry's theories captivated a news-hungry public, smaller nuggets were being ignored. These included the testimony of Minnie Barber, a "Hallelujah lassie" from the Salvation Army Industrial Home for Young Women that existed just north of Lakeside Hall. While the Westwood home was described as a "palatial residence," an imposing brick structure that looked over Lake Ontario, to its rear was a home for impoverished women. Miss Barber had been sleeping on the south side of the home and had not heard the fatal shot. The detectives had not considered the fact that the home attracted an eclectic collection of impoverished young women to an otherwise staid middle-class neighborhood.

The inquest ground on for the next month with evidence heard every Monday evening. By the end of October it appeared that "developments were destructive rather than constructive, the authorities apparently being still groping in the dark for a motive, for a clue, in fact for everything." Everyone had an alibi and everyone had loved Frank. Public interest in this intractable mystery began to wane and crowds no longer came to watch Crown attorney Dewart try to ferret out evidence. But, for the long-suffering, there were occasional gems of unexpected information. Isaac Anderson, one of Frank's pals, was asked if he had ever heard of any improper conduct between Frank and a girl. "He answered that he had heard a story once."[7] What story? The Crown attorney passed on quickly when Anderson said that it was from more than a year past. Was Dewart's eagerness to spare the family from a possible unpleasant incident getting in the way of the search for relevant facts? Even though every witness swore that Frank was a sterling character, diligent reporters soon discovered that the Westwood family was not without its little flaws. "It was learned from a private source," reported the *News* "that the son who was married about five years ago had to hurry along the date in order to avoid a scandal," and further that "Frank, while to all appearances a model young man, had his own difficulties and secret vices."[8]

Even more curious was the recollection of the other Crown attorney, James W. Curry, of the taking of Frank Westwood's *ante-mortem* statement. Even though the family had discouraged the taking of the statement on Monday, Curry had stopped by to talk with Frank. It was then that the youth had said, "We fooled around the hall for a few minutes."[9] Had Frank actually recognized the person at the door or was he referring to the outing with his friends earlier in the evening? For whatever reason, Curry chose not to follow up on this bizarre comment. Curry then read into the record the dying statement in which Frank Westwood declared that he had unlocked the door that night and was confronted by a mustachioed man who wore a fedora. Frank further stated that he had once had some trouble with a man named Gus Clark, and the man who shot him looked like one of Clark's chums, David Low. After signing the statement he seemed to drift into a reverie and said, "Mum's the word."

Adding to the deepening mystery were the comments made to the detectives at Lakeside Hall on the night of October 6. Detective

Coroner R.B. Orr conducting the Westwood inquest, Toronto News, *Oct. 16, 1894.*

Charles Slemin had questioned Frank at length and asked him about his female friends. He appeared to get annoyed and blurted out, "You can't pump me." When it was apparent that the police wanted to go through his clothes, he begged them to desist. They conducted the search anyway but found nothing. As he lay on his bed still bleeding badly and barely conscious, Frank looked up and recognized one of the policemen, Sergeant Coombes from the Queen Street division. Leaning over to the sergeant, Frank asked, "Gus is in the cooler, isn't he?" The sergeant asked, "You mean Gus Clark?" Frank said, "Yes." The sergeant responded, "No, he is not arrested that I know of." Frank rejoined, "Then that settles it" and closed his eyes. "Do you think Gus shot you, Frank?" the policeman persisted. "No, I don't know," Frank replied. The youth then added that the shooter did look like Clark's friend, David Low. Coombes immediately arranged to have both men picked up for questioning.

Frank Westwood had associated with a number of peculiar characters on the lakefront among whom Gus Clark was only one. For the most part his boating comrades stayed true to his memory. Ed

Lennox, one of his companions on the fatal evening, stated that Frank had always led a "proper life" and he could give no reason why anyone would want to kill him. Gus Clark had attended each day of the inquest and on its final day, November 12, he gave a story that seemed to eliminate him as a suspect. He had known Frank for four years and had considered him a friend. As a number of witnesses could confirm, Clark had been asleep in his boardinghouse at the time of the incident. Yet another dead end.

The question of motive was one of the most maddening aspects of the case.[10] Theories beyond number were being put forward, but the central question remained, as the *Telegram* phrased it, "When the lad is a sturdy, fine-looking young fellow, free of all visible vice, and a favourite in the circle where he moves, the search for a motive becomes still harder." There was simply nothing to work with. Somewhat defensively, one of the final witnesses, Detective Slemin, swore that the police had, "followed up every clue that had been brought to their notice, and were at the present moment absolutely in the dark." The headline in the *Globe* was "Justice Baffled."

Every day details of the inquest were printed in the city's many dailies for the public loved the vicarious thrills of a murder mystery. They avidly followed details of the police investigation and, much like Henry Hornberry, advanced their own theories on the crime. It was an age when Canadians could not wait for the latest instalment of the Sherlock Holmes stories to come from the pen of Arthur Conan Doyle.[11] Nothing quite matched shadowy figures skulking about the dim streets of London as horse-drawn cabs clattered over the cobblestones. Now Torontonians had a genuine mystery of their own on the foggy shores of Lake Ontario. Only a criminal of fiendish brilliance could have committed this act, an act which left the city's police completely baffled. The only difference between the Westwood tragedy and an Arthur Conan Doyle story was that no brilliant detective had emerged to apply cold logic to solve the problem.

In yet another bizarre twist, reporters from the Toronto *World* assembled all available articles on the Westwood mystery, mailed them to the famous novelist and asked for his considered opinion.[12] To Doyle's credit, he replied that he was a writer of mysteries and not a real police detective, for "I have never shown any special cleverness at resolving mysteries other than imaginary ones." Even the creator of Sherlock Holmes could offer no solution. A copy of the Conan Doyle letter was reprinted in the newspaper.

By the evening of November 12, Coroner Orr had decided to bring the proceedings to a close. He summed up the evidence that every person the police had talked to could give an account of their activities. No one could think of a motive for murdering Frank. The police simply had no answers. The jury issued a verdict that Frank Westwood had died from a bullet wound from the hand "of an unknown person." Coroner Orr "feared the probability of ever clearing up the terrible mystery was very slight."

CHAPTER THREE

Queen City

The mystery of Frank Westwood's murder was particularly compelling as the Toronto of the 1890s prided itself on being such a peaceful, law-abiding community. In 1893 there had only been one murder in this city of almost 200,000.[1] Frank's killing was the only premeditated murder of 1894. There were about thirty burglaries every year, but Chief Constable, H.J. Grasett, reassured the public that the amounts taken were small. At the Westwood inquest, Sergeant Hart had testified on the lack of any police presence in Parkdale and that there were no patrols south of King Street. It was such a quiet area that constables were not required. Those passing through Toronto remarked that it was a city of spires, where Methodist, Presbyterian and Anglican churches sent towers to the sky, monuments to their belief in God, the British Empire and Public Morality. The Sabbath was strictly observed and after services the truly devout attended temperance meetings to pray that the scourge of liquor might be completely expunged. For this reason, by the 1890s the city had acquired the sardonic title of "Toronto the Good."

If the city had little real crime, it seemed intent on fabricating some. Municipal reformers hoped to reduce the number of licensed taverns and stamp out the unknown scores of "groggeries" that operated outside the law. When William Howland became Toronto's mayor in 1886,[2] he tried to instill purity and virtue into the municipal administration and the following year the number of tavern licenses was cut from 223 to 150. In a New York speech, Mayor Howland proudly boasted that his city, "Kept the Sabbath and excluded from it the rum-sellers." On one occasion, Howland's enforcer of public morality, Staff Inspector David Archibald, conducted a public tour (accompanied by reporters) of some of the city's bordellos.[3] After shaming the customers and driving them out onto the streets, he proclaimed that Toronto had less of this "social evil" than any other comparably sized North American city. Still, prostitution was widespread, a condition that many attributed to the low salaries paid to working women. On another level, municipal reform seemed directed to enforcing a rigorous puritanism. Not only were the number of licensed taverns and their hours under police review, by January of 1894, Toronto considered a bylaw to close all bars after 9 p.m. Such a law, the *Globe* primly noted, would induce the working man "to get home at a reasonable hour, and be better fitted for his work next day." However a leading cleric objected and instead wanted, "to close all the saloons entirely, for all time."

Neither were the saloons the only source of evil. In the spring of 1895, the Toronto *World* complained of a recent show in which, "as the week progressed the exhibition became perfectly rank and putrid. Indecent handbills were distributed through the city informing men and boys of the character of the exhibition." The *World* entitled this scandalous report as "Where was Inspector Archibald?" Usually the police were very much in evidence. Bylaws prohibiting ball-playing on Sunday and forbidding boys from swimming naked in the bay were duly enforced. Indeed, the Toronto police seemed to take to heart their role as protectors of public morality. Social observer, C.S. Clark, in his notorious book, *Of Toronto the Good*, asked if the police were really acting appropriately when an eleven-year-old boy was charged with playing with a rubber ball on a Sunday and fined two dollars or ten days in jail.[4] Clark thought, "The city has something else to do with its money than to pay policemen to run down children who in their innocence think it no sin to try and enjoy themselves." On occasion, posters of scantily clad ballet artists were posted on city streets but the police were on the case and, in his annual report for 1894, Chief Constable H.J. Grasett assured the public that "theatrical posters ... considered indecent" were taken down and those responsible prosecuted. The policeman's lot was not always a happy one, for they were often seen as spoilsports for administering unpopular and puritanical codes.

While Toronto's first police contingents of the 1830s resembled the parish watch who used to protect English villages, by the 1890s they had been replaced by a professional force.[5] Uniformed, drilled and equipped with modern handguns and equipment, the Toronto police compared favourably to any American force. Since his appointment as inspector of detectives in 1887, William Stark had campaigned for a separate investigation section and it was thanks to his efforts that the Department of Detectives was created in 1892.[6] This enabled investigators to photograph criminals and eventually introduce the cutting edge of forensic technology, the Bertillon system for the registration of the key facial and bodily dimensions of criminals.[7] This system required the police to record eleven body measurements such as height, arm span and length of hand. As these measurements were rarely, if ever, exactly duplicated, criminals could not change identity and evade the police. Stark was immensely proud of this innovation and in 1897, using Crown attorney Curry as the subject, he gave a public display of "Bertillonage."

A Toronto Police Constable, 1887. Courtesy of the Toronto Police Museum.

On the streets, the Toronto police often were forced to handle confrontations between Irish Protestants and Catholics. These Orange-Green riots in the 1870s and 1880s had simmered down by the 1890s, but the police still had to show their impartiality between ethnic groups and their determination to maintain public order. In some ways, the police were a foreign element in the city. As Nicholas Rogers observed, the police "were segregated from the mainstream of working-class life."[8] They lived near each other in respectable neighbourhoods and tended to be Irish-born Protestants who had seen service in either the British military or police. As the level of violent crime and robberies was small, the police spent much of their efforts on clearing the streets of drunks and prostitutes and enforcing the Sabbatarian laws. Leaving horses untied, goods on the sidewalks or awnings too low were all offences that could and did result in citizens visiting the Police Court. Indeed, the police seemed to regard enforcement with considerable gusto for the chief constable crowed in his annual report for 1895 that, "It is with much pleasure that I can report the closing of the pool rooms." This generated negative feelings towards the enforcers and the *World* felt that the cost of policing was exorbitant and that Toronto's taxpayers were spending far more than those in comparable cities in the United States. "The citizens are constantly worried by petty tyrannical by-laws and then taxed to death for the cost of enforcing them," the *World* editorialists moaned.[9] But perhaps this excessive police cost was necessary, they suggested tongue-in-cheek, as Toronto's police "are expected to do much more; they are required to enforce:

1.   2,200 city by-laws.
2.   The Ten Commandments
3.   Amendments to the Ten Commandments."

It was a measure of Toronto's tranquility that the issue of the day in the summer of 1893 was whether or not streetcars[10] should be

A typical Toronto sweatshop of the 1890s. Courtesy of the Toronto Public Library.

permitted to operate on Sundays. The majority of the clergy was resolutely against it and thought that the Sabbath should be used for worship and then in quiet reflection. A *Globe* reporter toured the parks on a Sunday and found them heavily used, particularly the area south of "the new Parliament Buildings, generally styled 'at the guns,'" and that streetcars were not needed for these pursuits. On the other hand, the *World* lobbied for Sunday streetcars for as matters stood, on their one day off, working-class families were trapped in the city "stifling for want of pure air." The streetcars were an essential feature of modern life and by the 1890s the promiscuous hum of traffic was regularly heard on the major thoroughfares. The main King Street cross-town car, the same one operated by Samuel Sherwood on the night of October 6, enabled rich and poor to move rapidly across the city.

The burgeoning streetcar system was another indication of Toronto's emergence as the industrial hub of Ontario. Since the 1880s the city had become known as the "Queen City," the focus of commercial growth and expansion. Packing plants, distillers and farm equipment manufacturers had all invested heavily in the city and the 530 manufacturers of 1871 had become 2,401 by 1891. The general rise in industrial activity had carried along with it an unprecedented commercial expansion. Toronto became the wholesaler to Ontario and to the expanding Canadian west. Its merchants sold goods not only to the local market but also across the province and to new markets in the prairies. Benjamin Westwood, as a manufacturer and retailer of fishing gear, was just one example of the specialized trade that characterized the Queen City. The elder Westwood had been born in England and, as a young man, had joined the Allcock fishing tackle firm. In 1868, when Benjamin and his wife Clara emigrated to Canada, he started a branch of the firm in Toronto. Allcock, Leight and Westwood quickly became one of the prime suppliers of fishing gear in the city and across the province.[11]

Mr. Westwood's town of Parkdale, described by the *Globe* as a "well-to-do residential retreat," was annexed to Toronto in 1889. This was just part of a process that saw the size of the city almost double during the 1880s. By 1894 the police census estimated the city's size as 194,000.[12] In that year a housing shortage was reported and there were practically no vacancies "in the north end and in Parkdale." Unlike most American cities, Toronto did not draw its workers from foreign sources. Rather, there was a huge migration of surplus farm labour from the countryside and substantial immigration from the British Isles. From overseas came thousands of English, Irish and Scots who added to the overwhelmingly British Protestant tone of Victorian Toronto. "How English is Toronto!" exclaimed G. Mercer Adam, in 1891, "English speech and English ways are the characteristics of our people."[13] One of the political debates of the day concerned whether Canada should become independent of Britain or join the United States. Colonel George T. Denison, a police magistrate, imperialist and leading figure in

Toronto society, once declared at a dinner party that he was vehemently opposed to either independence or annexation, and if such distasteful topics were ever seriously considered, "I would only argue it in one way, and that was on horseback with my sword."

Despite its puritanism and imperial enthusiasms, the Toronto of 1894 was a strikingly modern city. Electric streetcars took thousands of passengers to work at modern factories or to shop at some of the largest department stores on the continent. At night, electric arc lights illuminated intersections where uniformed police stood guard. The Queen City offered a wide array of theatrical and social occasions. Just days before the Westwood tragedy, high society was preparing for the unveiling of the statute of Sir John A. Macdonald at Queen's Park. All senior members of the judiciary attended, including Ontario's Chancellor John Boyd. For lesser folk, there were other amusements. In August 1894, Toronto's small Black community held its annual celebration of Emancipation Day and "about 100 of these worthy citizens" attended. A month later, "Moore's Musée" put on an exhibition of trained wolves including "rope-walking wolves, somersault wolves, leapers, dancers" and wild hyenas.[14] Rather incongruously, this pack of performing brutes was followed by the "world's greatest pedal pianist," Miss Lizzie Sturgeon. In the first week in October, Jacobs and Sparrow's Opera House featured a new play "in all its superlative excellence" called *The Black Crook*.

CHAPTER FOUR

"You Know My Color"

Of all the boathouse crowd, Gus Clark had been the most stung by being named during the inquest, and he knew that until the mystery was solved that he remained under suspicion. A free-spirited individual, Clark had fought in the Northwest Rebellion of 1885[1] with Toronto's Royal Grenadiers. After the conflict, he was unable to settle down and in 1889 he again tried his luck in the Northwest. Disappointed, he had drifted back to Ontario's north country. Crown attorney Dewart had advanced him twenty dollars to pay for his travel back to Toronto, but Clark had spent the money to finance a binge in his hometown.[2]

One item to come out of the inquest had piqued Clark's interest. He recalled W.H. Hornberry's thesis that the killer could be a woman dressed up as a man. However preposterous the police may have considered this notion, it spurred Clark to recall that one of his female acquaintances had frequently dressed and passed herself off as a man. This exotic creature had lived in a shanty next to the Salvation Army refuge and she was well known to the others in the boathouse crowd, including Ed Lennox and Frank Westwood. Moreover, she was known to carry a revolver and was of an unpredictable and, at times, violent disposition. Even more outstanding in this overwhelmingly white society was that she was of mixed race, a mulatto. Gus Clark told police investigators how the boys in the neighbourhood (including Frank Westwood) had occasionally teased her and how she had deeply resented their taunts. On one occasion, she had frightened Clark's sisters to the extent that they had called the police who subsequently placed her under surveillance. However strange her appearance in this most conformist of societies, nothing she had done justified the law's intervention.

Her name was Clara Ford.

The detectives on the case, Charles Slemin and George Porter, became aware of Clark's suspicions. The two detectives were typical of the Toronto force.[3] Both were Irish-born Protestants and Porter had served for several years in the Canadian military before joining the police. On their first attempt to locate Clara, they failed to find any trace of her. However, one thing they did learn was that she was especially close to another mixed-race girl named Florence or Flora McKay. It was rumoured that this Flora was her daughter and if they found her she might well lead them to the suspect. Entire sections of the city were searched until on Tuesday, November 20, they found Flora, a fifteen-year-old girl, working as a servant for a family on Jarvis Street. Without saying why they wanted her, the detectives asked after Clara and were told that she worked at a tailor's shop on York Street. Slemin and Porter also took the opportunity to ask Flora what she knew about the events of October 6. The timid girl described for them how both she and Clara had gone to the Opera House to see *The Black Crook* that evening. The answer seemed a little too rehearsed and both men asked her repeatedly where she had

York Street looking north, 1856. The address, 154 York, is about mid-picture. Osgood Hall is seen in the background. Courtesy of the City of Toronto Archives, Fonds 1498, Item 16.

gone that night. At last, she broke down and told the detectives that she had arranged to meet with Clara but that the later had not shown up. During the following week, Clara had instructed Flora to tell anyone who asked that they had been together at the Opera House.

Samuel Barnett's tailor shop at 154 York Street was the next stop for detectives Slemin and Porter. They now found themselves in a different world from Parkdale. St. John's Ward, usually just called "the Ward," lay in the heart of the city north of Queen Street and west of Yonge.[4] Ever since the 1850s it had been the poorest of Toronto's seven wards. Still, at mid-century it had been overwhelmingly British, Protestant and respectably working-class. However, as the century wore on, the Ward increasingly attracted Toronto's small community of outsiders, Jews, Blacks and the poor. Clara Ford lived barely a block south of the stately law courts at Osgoode Hall. However York Street was anything but stately. Rather, it was a hodgepodge of small Jewish shops including Tugenhaft grocers, Rabinowich the watchmaker, and Lepovsky and Berman butchers. Photographs of the Ward during this period show it to be an unruly collection of run-down one- or two-storey structures. Located incongruently in the midst of this teeming Jewish block was a fixture of Toronto's small Black community, Chloe Dorsay's restaurant. Mrs. Dorsay's place was where the community came to gossip and where American friends travelling through town would stay and be welcome. Clara rented a small room over the restaurant. While, to its residents, the Ward was home, it was also a troubled landscape, traversed during the day by servants and seamstresses and at night by prostitutes and drunks.

Slemin and Porter found Clara in the basement working at a sewing machine. She was a competent seamstress, her employer noted, who was diligent about her work and rarely took a day off. Today would be an exception for the officers explained that the chief of detectives, Inspector Stark himself, wanted a word with her. Before setting out, the detectives asked if they could see her room. She acquiesced and, once in her tiny bedroom, Porter asked if she had any men's clothing. After hesitating for a moment, Clara responded that she did and opened a trunk and pulled out a man's suit. It was not stolen, she hastened to advise the officers. She was then asked if she had a revolver and, opening another trunk, brought out a .38 calibre pistol. There were also four cartridges. According to Clara, she had expended two others shooting at ducks. As the party prepared to leave for the police station, Clara blurted out an unsolicited declaration that was guaranteed to arouse the suspicions of the dullest investigator, "Oh, it's the Westwood case you mean. I can prove where I was that night. I was at the Toronto Opera House and the play was *The Black Crook*."

Nothing further was said, neither was Clara given any warning that she faced a criminal charge. At about four in the afternoon, she was brought into the station and seated in the office of the senior investigator, Sergeant of Detectives Henry Reburn.[5]

The sergeant began by warning her that anything she might say would be used against her and that she was a suspect in the murder

Inspector William Stark.
Courtesy of the Toronto
Police Museum.

of Frank Westwood. "I never knew him," she replied, "I was at the theatre that night and I have evidence to prove I was there."[6] Reburn asked her for her proof and she replied that the girl, Flora McKay, would back up her story. Porter was called in and told to go pick up Flora. Turning back to his suspect, Reburn repeated his caution and then asked where she had gone after the theatre. She went home, she replied, and was in her own room a little after ten. In exasperation, she volunteered that she did not even know Frank Westwood and Reburn would soon realize that he was interrogating the wrong person. While Reburn continued to talk with Clara, more details emerged. She was friendly with another woman, Mary Crozier, and Clara had given a black fedora (similar to the one worn by the shooter) to one of the Crozier children. Reburn ordered that Mrs. Crozier be brought in as well. It was now about 6:30 and Reburn suggested that Clara have dinner in the matron's room. In the meantime, Flora had arrived and Reburn satisfied himself that her story was irreconcilable with Clara's.

At 7:15 they started again. Reburn decided to move the interrogation to Inspector Stark's office and confronted her that she had never gone to the theatre that night. Flora was brought in and asked where she was on the night of October 6. The girl confirmed that she was supposed to meet up with Clara but that she had never come and that later Clara had told her to lie and say that they had gone to the show. At this, Clara turned angrily towards Flora, but Reburn stopped her and warned Clara that anything she said could be used against her. Once Flora was taken out, Clara regained her composure and said that the girl was scattered and that she was just unable to remember the events. Did she have any other witnesses Reburn asked? There were none.

Reburn left the room for a moment, and when he returned he told Clara that Mary Crozier was waiting in an antechamber and that her story would also contradict Clara's alibi. "She will not say it to my face," a defiant Clara insisted. Yet Mrs. Crozier simply repeated her recollection of the evening, that Clara Ford had been at their house till 9 o'clock or shortly thereafter and had then announced that she was going to Parkdale to pick up Flora and go to the show. Clara rounded on her friend until Reburn stepped in and reminded her, "Hold on, you are on trial for your life and I don't want you to say anything." Crozier continued that Clara was carrying a revolver that night. "It's all lies," Clara erupted "It's untrue." But Mrs. Crozier's daughter corroborated her mother's story. Both of the Crozier women were then allowed to leave. By now, a number of reporters had heard the news that there might be an arrest in the Westwood case and there was an excited buzz in the lobby of the station. For greater privacy, Reburn decided to move the interrogation into the most inaccessible part of police headquarters, the commissioner's room. He was entirely unprepared for what was about to happen next.

The door to the commissioner's room had barely closed when Clara turned to Sergeant Reburn and said, "There is no use in misleading you any longer in this matter." Reburn asked her what she meant and reminded her yet again that anything she said could be

'I SHOT FRANK WESTWOOD'

Clara Ford's Confession to Detective-Sergeant Reburn.

"A BULLET FOR THE BOY, ANOTHER FOR DUCKS."

Headline "Parkdale Relieved," Toronto Empire, *Nov. 27, 1894.*

taken down as evidence against her. "Well, I don't care," she responded, "I deserve what I get. If you had a sister and she was treated the way I was treated, you would treat him the same way." She took in a breath.

"I shot Frank Westwood."

The first question that came to Reburn was the most intriguing: Why? Clara was about to give him a story that would significantly alter sympathies. "About the end of August or about last July," she explained "he got hold of me at the foot of Jameson Avenue, and he tried to knock me down and take improper liberties with me. I told him I would get even with him. The boys had been teasing me. I was in the habit of getting down and sitting at the boathouse reading and you know how colored people are called names."

The sergeant then extracted from her a detailed account of how she had carried out the killing. From the central city she had walked past Gurney's Foundry to the intersection of Dominion and Dufferin streets. There she took off her skirt and jacket and hid them under the sidewalk. Dressed in the man's clothing she had on underneath, she proceeded along side streets to Jameson and through a hole in the picket fence up to the Westwood mansion. She hid behind a tree trying to discern who was in the house. After seeing Frank take leave of his companions and go in, she waited about twenty minutes before going up and ringing the doorbell. She noticed the dim light in the hall. When Frank opened the door she fired the one shot. "I did not intend to kill him" she told Reburn, "I never dreamt that I was going to kill him." Reburn asked if Frank had recognized her. "I don't think so," she replied and she seemed sorry that she had done the deed. Still, she added, "Any man who attempts to take an advantage of a woman deserves it." In this almost manipulative way, the premeditated killing of a youth was being transformed into justifiable act of revenge, a preservation of honour. Thereafter she had retraced her steps back to Dominion Street where she put on her female clothes and continued along the lakefront under the wharves. She went past the New Fort, just east of the Exhibition Grounds, crossed the commons and from there to the downtown.

By this point, interrogator and subject had achieved a degree of understanding, a mutual interest in establishing just what had happened. Reburn remained curious as to why she had waited before acting. "If you had done it at the time (of the assault) he would have deserved it and you would have deserved credit for doing it." Reburn suggested helpfully, "Why did you not take him to court?"

"Well," she said "You know my color; I would have no chance with a man in a case like that." Added to her story of defending feminine dignity was yet another layer, that as a poor Black seamstress, she had no other option, that society would inevitably have taken the side of a white boy from a respectable family against hers.

Flora McKay was brought in again and Clara told her that it was all over and that she could tell the truth. "Don't you remember me telling you I was at Parkdale that night?" The girl denied it and seemed to be hopelessly confused. Sergeant Reburn again intervened and said that she was doing her best to recall, "You're stupid," Clara concluded, "or you have got mixed."

Just to ensure that the confession was correctly taken down,

Clara Ford became an instant news-paper sensation, Toronto *World, Nov. 22, 1894.*

Reburn took Clara to Inspector Stark who wrote down her statement. By nine that evening she was formally charged with the murder of Frank Westwood.

The following day all of Toronto's dailies carried the electric news of the arrest and the elusive emotions of the public were once again captivated by the Westwood case. "Did She Kill Him? - Inspector Stark Confident That He Has An Unbreakable Chain Of Evidence" was the lead headline in the day's edition of the Toronto *Star*.[7] There were detailed, if frequently inaccurate, accounts of the investigation. The *Globe* noted that the public had almost lost interest in the Westwood case until "the fresh sensation consequent on the arrest of the mulatto man-woman" sparked an even more intense curiosity.

Most of the dailies suggested that Clara Ford had confessed to the crime, but for the time being the police remained tight-lipped. Yet it was the revelation of a motive that created the greatest sensation. To some, it appeared that the spirit of the deceased Frank Westwood was now on trial. Was he a violent rapist whom many Torontonians would consider got what he deserved? It was a time when the honour of a respectable woman was considered almost sacred, and the allegation that Frank Westwood had tried to sexually assault a woman created a tangle of legal and moral issues that created doubt as to just who was the victim. While there was absolutely no corroboration of Clara's story, some in the press accepted it without question. The *Globe* presumed that it was true for "there is little reason to doubt its truth" and the story did seem to give her the moral high ground for her explanation of the motive did "not reflect credit on the reputation of the youth whose life was so ruthlessly cut short."[8] In contrast, the *World* thought that an unwarrantable insult had been levied against the dead and reminded *Globe* readers that the reputation of a fine young man from one of the city's leading families was also at stake. The *Globe* hastened to retract its earlier pronouncement and advised its readers to suspend judgment on the truthfulness, if any, on Clara Ford's explanation of her motives. Whatever these motives were, there was no question, wrote the *Globe*, that this tragedy was one of the "saddest, and at the same time most sensational that ever figured in the police annals of Toronto."

The sensation was just beginning.

CHAPTER FIVE

A Complete Solution

During the early days of her incarceration there developed a strange rapport between the sergeant and the seamstress. On the morning after the arrest, Reburn had Clara taken up to that part of the station used by the detectives as a bedroom. In this intimate area he had a tête-à-tête with her about her prospects. "My time is short," was her estimate. Reburn protested that the charge would have to be proven and urged her to get a lawyer. She refused, "A lawyer will do me no good. I am going to tell the court when I go in." Reburn pressed her to reconsider, "You have told me you did not intend to kill him and that will be a question for the jury. You will be on your trial for murder, and if you plead guilty of murder before the magistrate you will be hung... you take my advice and get a lawyer." Still, she seemed resigned to her fate. "No, I don't want no lawyer," she insisted. For a person with as much stubborn pride as Clara Ford, the prospect of being found out again as a liar and cheat, this time on a public witness stand, might have seemed worse than death.

After further pleas from the sergeant, she relented and asked him to suggest the names of some competent lawyers.[1] Among others, he mentioned W.G. Murdoch, or if he was unavailable, to get Murphy. She settled on Murdoch, and Reburn immediately arranged to have him brought to the station to interview his new client. This solicitous attitude, which Reburn might not have been so quick to display had the accused murderer been a man, was setting the tone for much of what was to follow.

Later that morning Clara Ford was brought to Colonel Denison's Police Court to face her arraignment for the murder of Frank Westwood. A great crowd buzzed in and around the courtroom, eager to hear the details of the charge. As she appeared in court for the first time "her dusky countenance displayed no indication of fear or emotion." A *Globe* reporter described her as a "tall, fine-looking woman, with neat, well-cut hair, well-cut features and but for her swarthy skin and short, curly, wooly hair, has few of the physical characteristics of the negro race."[2] The various descriptions of Clara Ford in the Toronto press emphasized the racial difference; that she was the "other" and not part of normal society. The *World* took this to a heightened level when they described her appearance in the Police Court: "It could easily be seen that she had a strong dash of negro blood in her, being probably a quadroon or nearer to the black. Her curved nose shows the white strain, while her restless eyes and sensuous mouth tell of her African origins. Her complexion is between a chocolate and an unhealthy yellow." Invariably, all the newspapers would refer to her as "dusky" in appearance.

Colonel George T. Denison, the presiding magistrate, prepared to read the indictment against her. Denison, the virtual monarch of Toronto's Police Court, was an imperious magistrate who despised technicalities, conducted cases at breakneck speed, and tended to rely on his intuition to decide guilt or innocence.[3] It was said that

Clara Ford in the dock, in custody on the charge of murdering Frank Westwood. Sketch by H.M. Russell, Toronto News, *Nov. 21, 1894.*

tourists considered a visit to Toronto incomplete without attending Denison's court, that it "would be like going to Rome and not seeing the Pope." Usually his court was a carnival of the picaresque, featuring a steady parade of pickpockets, drunks and prostitutes. But this Wednesday morning the Colonel's court was held in deadly earnest. Denison read off the charge in stern tones and asked the prisoner how she would plead.

In a clear voice Clara Ford responded, "Guilty."

Stillness came over the room, as if for a moment everyone was spellbound. She had just pled guilty to a crime that mandated death by hanging. Yet her pride was such that, as she had promised Sergeant Reburn, "I am going to tell the court when I go in." And she had been as good as her word. Still, the court could not accept a plea of guilty to a capital offence. W.G. Murdoch sprang from his seat and began to whisper into her ear. Denison repeated the question and the intervening silence became even more intense. This time Clara decided to play their game and called out, "Not Guilty." She was bound over to a preliminary hearing.

A week later she again appeared before the magistrate and again her languid demeanour made her seem the calmest person in the courtroom. Appearing almost by sleight of hand, she made her way up an interior stairway to the prisoner's dock in the midst of a teeming courtroom. Once there, she "sat with half-closed eyes and languid mien, with absolutely no expression of interest or anxiety upon her dusky features." According to another report she "sat in the dock yesterday while the story was being unfolded in all its revolting details without displaying the slightest emotion." She was quite possibly the calmest person in the building. Nor was this the usual collection of Police Court hangers-on. Instead, the crowd was composed of "clergymen, curates, law and medical students" as well as an unusual number of ladies.[4] They were eager to hear the Crown's case and, for the first time, to hear details of the confession.

City Crown attorney Curry conducted the preliminary hearing before Colonel Denison who would be joined by Toronto's mayor, Warring Kennedy (who was facing an election in five weeks and needed as much public exposure as he could get), and several other justices of the peace. Curry had Mrs. Westwood and Dr. Lynd recount the events of October 6. Dressed in mourning, her faced creased with sorrow, Mrs. Westwood described yet again her last intimate chat with her son. Strangely enough, both she and Dr. Lynd recognized Clara Ford. Mrs. Westwood recalled when she had lived next to the Clark place and Dr. Lynd had attended Clara's foster mother, Mrs. McKay. In response to one of Murdoch's questions, Lynd did add one intriguing footnote. Just after making the *ante-mortem* statement Frank Westwood had wistfully added, "mum's the word." Lynd understood this to mean that he hesitated to implicate Gus Clark. Or was there something about the incident that even the victim did not want made public?

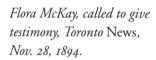

Flora McKay, called to give testimony, Toronto News, Nov. 28, 1894.

Benjamin Westwood took the stand and held up the still blood-soaked vest his son had worn that night. For once, Clara averted her eyes and looked at the bank of reporters instead of the witness.[5] The prosecution was working its way up to proving the charge and was saving its most vital witnesses for the last. Next on the stand was Florence McKay. Flora, like her putative mother, was a tall, good-looking girl, described by the press as "well-grown for her age, and showing only slight traces of the colored blood in her veins." As with Clara, Flora's racial appearance would be a continual subject of newspaper references. Flora had known the prisoner "ever since I can remember." She recounted the story of the false alibi, but added a new twist when she reported that about a week after the killing Clara had mentioned to Flora that she was in Parkdale on the night of the shooting:

"Did you have any conversation with her?

"Just a few words. She said she told me that she was in Parkdale on Saturday night and not to say anything about her being there."

Flora readily admitted that she thought the police were after

Clara for the killing of Frank Westwood and she would do what she could to protect her. Curry asked:

"What made you think the detectives would think Clara shot Frank Westwood?

"I thought that right away," Flora responded. "That was what I thought."

"Why did you think that?" he continued.

"Because I knew she dressed up in men's clothes." she replied.

Curry continued to press her on the source of her knowledge, "What made you think the detectives would think Clara Ford shot Frank Westwood?"

She replied that she did not know if Clara was acquainted with Frank Westwood. Then she added, that she knew Frank but had not seen him since her family had left Parkdale three years since. To Murdoch, Flora stated that the detectives did not cow her. He then suggested to her that much of her testimony was derived from newspaper accounts. She denied it.

Mary Crozier, one of Clara Ford's closest friends was the next to testify. They had met when Mary had been a cashier at the Temperance League Coffee House where Clara had worked as a waitress. Mary was chummy enough with her that she had frequently teased Clara on her masculine appearance, a chaffing that Clara accepted, and had once caused Clara to remark, "she thought a mistake had been made that she was not born a boy. She would rather be a man than a woman." Clara regularly stopped off at the Croziers' on Saturdays to pick up her laundry. On the evening of October 6 she had arrived about eight o'clock and had chatted with the family. While Clara was usually most abstemious, Mary Crozier noted that she appeared to be a little tipsy that evening. About an hour after her arrival she announced that she was off to Parkdale to meet Flora and go to a show. Just before leaving, one of the Crozier children pulled back her coat and exclaimed, "Oh, Clara has got a revolver!" The following week Clara came by as usual. Mary Crozier brought out a newspaper account of the Westwood tragedy and Clara asked to see the paper. After looking at it she commented, "I am glad I was not there or I would be blamed for it." About the same time Clara gave a fedora to Mary for the children to play with.

The day was wearing on to twilight when the Crown finally called its principal witnesses. Charles Slemin entered the witness box and described how he and Porter had seized Clara at Barnett's tailor shop, asked her for her male clothing, and deposited her at the police station. They had barely begun to talk with her when she had become defensive. Before anyone had even accused her of anything, or even so much as mentioned the Westwood case, she denied any involvement. Murdoch began to lay the groundwork for the defence when he raised objections as to Slemin's recollections of Clara's comments. "Was she under arrest at the time she spoke?" he asked. Slemin could not give a precise answer. The officers would not have released her, but neither had she been arrested nor cautioned. Still, they had been careful not to ask her about the Westwood case. But the most important evidence of the day would come from Sergeant of Detectives Henry Reburn.

The sergeant recounted the course of the interrogation and how Clara had denied any involvement until, piece-by-piece, Reburn had dismantled her alibi. Along the way he had cautioned her not once but on several occasions that anything she said could be used against her. Despite these warnings she had insisted on giving him differing accounts of the events until at last, with her alibi in tatters, she felt obliged to admit that she was the killer and talked of pleading guilty. According to the Toronto *Empire,* "That the statement astonished every one within hearing distance – that the prisoner not only made a full and complete confession of the crime, but insisted on doing so in open court. She was only persuaded to act otherwise by both the sergeant and Inspector Stark." When he asked her why she did it, "She told me the way they teased her and tantalized her. She could not live up there (Parkdale) on account of her color, she said. It was no fun to be dressed in man's clothes and she always carried a revolver for protection."

Two days before the preliminary hearing, Reburn and Inspector Stark had walked the route as described by Clara. Along the way they noted the holes under the sidewalk at Dufferin Street where she hid her skirt and blouse and the gap in the picket fence around Lakeside Hall, which she had used for an entrance. It took about fifty minutes to walk the distance from the Crozier's house on Camden Street to Jameson. The *Globe* reporter felt that Reburn's testimony was the high point of the proceeding and that it was "listened to in breathless silence by the densely crowded court." It was the nature of the confession that captivated the crowd for "So terrible and minute a confession has seldom, if ever, been heard in a Canadian court of justice, and a feeling almost akin to awe oppressed the listeners." According to a reporter from the Toronto *Telegram*, as Reburn recounted the taking of the confession, Clara fixed him with a stare. But this did not last long and "gradually her gaze wandered farther and farther away until she seemed to be gazing out the window into the dusk of the fall twilight."[6]

As for Henry Reburn, the testimony seemed to be a painful duty. He appeared to be uncomfortable on the stand, especially when Murdoch asked him why, several days after the arrest, he had talked with Clara about whether or not she was Florence McKay's mother. "This has nothing to do with the case," suggested Murdoch.

"You are right, it has not," admitted the sergeant. He then added that on this occasion, Clara stated that the police had the wrong person. To some, it might appear that the sergeant was overly sympathetic to this prisoner. Yet, other than making a formal objection to the confession, Murdoch held back from any detailed examination of Reburn. That Clara Ford would stand trial was a foregone conclusion and there was no purpose served in enlightening the prosecution on defence tactics.

Henry Reburn had barely gotten out of the witness box when Colonel Denison announced that the prisoner would be remanded for trial at the next assizes.

To most observers, Clara Ford's fate seemed preordained. She would be convicted of murder and the only serious question was whether or not she would receive any clemency that would spare her the rope. Little over twenty years previously, in 1873, Elizabeth Workman of Sarnia had gone to the gallows for murdering her husband.[7] Despite the fact that the victim was an alcoholic who often abused and threatened Elizabeth, she was convicted and failed to obtain a pardon. Even though she had the support of the Sarnia *Observer*, which argued that she was the victim of a tyrannical husband, Elizabeth Workman, clutching a bouquet of white flowers, went to the gallows. There was no guarantee that Clara Ford could rely on her sex to save her from the same fate. However, she had already raised two powerful pleas, that of the wronged woman defending her honour and that of the poor victim of racial intolerance. It remained to be seen how effective these would be.

What was apparent was that the Toronto police had resolved a mystery that only a few days before had seemed beyond solution. Chief Constable Grasett's yearly report cited the Ford case for "One crime of this nature (murder) was committed under circumstances of mysterious perplexity, baffling for a time the strenuous efforts put forth by the detective staff to discover the perpetrators... A woman charged with the offence has been arrested and now awaits trial." The *Globe* congratulated the detectives for their excellent work.[8] They singled out Slemin and Porter "and it is largely owing to their painstaking and intelligent work that what at one time threatened to be an unsolved mystery now gives promise of complete solution." The *Mail* also saluted both detectives "whose persistence and intelligent management of the case generally are deserving of the highest praise."

It is one of the great ironies of the Clara Ford affair that over the next few months the public perception of the police, the prisoner and the deceased would evolve and become very different from these first impressions.

CHAPTER SIX

Clara

By now, Clara Ford was an object of almost limitless speculation. All Toronto wanted to know who she was and where she came from. They were about to get a very mixed picture.

Some said that she was a foundling, while others were convinced that she was the offspring of a liaison between the white son of a respectable family and a Black serving girl. The *Globe* accepted this later explanation as "the more generally accepted statement and the one which there is little doubt is correct" and besides, it added a romantic tinge to the story that *Globe* readers would be sure to enjoy. By talking to those who knew her, diligent reporters from the *World* found out that Clara had been deposited at the home of a Mrs. Stow in about 1862. Nothing certain was known of the identity of either her father or mother, but it seems most likely that she was indeed the daughter of a Black serving girl and a white man. In later years, Mrs. Stow's two granddaughters recalled her relating the strange "circumstances of the finding of the foundling on her doorstep." Mrs. Stow tried to leave the infant at the Foundlings' Nursery (whose matron gave the child her surname of "Ford") but a raging illness at the institution required the Stows to resume their burden. They then arranged for one of the family's servants, Mrs. Jessie McKay, to look after Clara. For some years, the Stows paid for her upkeep, but this eventually ceased. Nevertheless, Mrs. McKay, a childless widow from Quebec took to Clara and raised her as her own. This report seems to be in general agreement with the only census account for Clara in 1871 where she is listed as being seven years old and living with Mrs. McKay.[1]

The two lived in poverty, moving from shanty to shanty until finally settling on Gloucester Street where Mrs. McKay took in laundry and used any edge she could to make do. For example, while Mrs. McKay passed herself off as Presbyterian, they also attended St. Luke's Anglican church and made a few pennies washing surplices for that congregation. John Hoskin, a prominent lawyer, recalled that Mrs. McKay had done his household cleaning and laundry during the 1870s and that she was always accompanied by a little Black girl who "was always ugly if spoken to about her color."[2] Clara went to the Park Street School, and her experiences there may have shaped her disposition. A former schoolmate recalled, "because of her color and the mystery surrounding her birth the child was practically ostracized... the children of the school kept aloof from her."[3] Not surprisingly, "This treatment had a marked effect upon the girl's disposition, making her sullen and bad tempered." One of the few members of Toronto's Black community who knew her, her landlady Chloe Dorsay, later recounted how Clara "would not associate with the negro class in which she was usually assigned membership. She felt herself above them." She had wanted to associate with whites even though "she was rather looked down upon and subjected to many little cuts and insults which

*Wilson Ruffin
Abbott (1801-1876)
brought his family
to Toronto from the
United States in
the mid-1830s.*
Courtesy of the
Abbott family.

grievously wounded her." Navigating this cold and alien world seemed to offer her little and, in her late teens or early twenties, she decided to try her luck across the border.

Whatever her exact origins, Clara Ford was a descendant of the Black community that had existed in Toronto since before the American Civil War. A few Blacks had lived in the capital since the 1790s, but it was only after the U.S. Congress passed the Fugitive Slave Act in 1850 that significant numbers of American Blacks began to seek refuge in Canada. Most of these refugees went to border towns such as Windsor or Chatham, but some ventured as far as Toronto while others went north to the Owen Sound and Collingwood areas. The 1860 census estimated that the city had a Black population of 510 with 366 of these resident in St. John's Ward and concentrated in the neighborhood known as "Macaulaytown." By the 1850s the

Black vote in Toronto was powerful enough to be courted by politicians and during the annual Emancipation Day celebrations office-seekers were known to work the crowds in search of favour. In addition to political rights, Blacks enjoyed limited educational and commercial opportunities. Wilson R. Abbott, who had to flee the American South in 1834, became a wealthy man in Toronto and one of the largest landowners in the ward. Prominent in local affairs, he was elected to Toronto City Council, instigated taxpayer petitions on public issues of concern to both Black and white residents and had served briefly on the organizing committee for the Canadian Anti-Slavery Society. His son, Anderson R. Abbott, was the first Canadian-born person of African ancestry to graduate from medical school in Toronto in 1861.[4]

Yet, there were hints that this toleration would not last. After 1865 the province's Black population declined as many refugees returned to their former homes. It was roughly estimated that half of Ontario's Black population of 40,000 re-emigrated to the United States. After the tumult of the Civil War, Robin Winks has noted that "Earlier postures of acceptance shown by whites could now turn to gestures of rejection... the Negro in Canada found himself sliding down an inclined plane from mere neglect to active dislike."[5] In most places in Ontario (but not in Toronto) Blacks were taught in separate schools and worshiped in their own churches. This attitude was apparent in Colonel Denison's Police Court of the 1890s where Black defendants were invariably viewed with suspicion or disdain. In his memoirs, Denison recalled that Blacks provided a "source of amusement in the court because of their many peculiarities" and he recounted several incidents (in a heavy minstrel dialect) where Black litigants were portrayed as either pompous or ignorant.[6] Therefore, when Clara Ford explained that there was no use complaining to the police for "You know my color, they wouldn't believe me," she was only stating a truism which was well known to both Blacks and whites. The word of a penniless Black woman would never be accepted over that of a respectable white man. It is even more revealing of Clara Ford's own sense of place that she was offended whenever she was referred to as "mulatto." She insisted that she was not of Black heritage at all, but that her father was "Spanish" and she insisted on being looked upon as such.[7] Mrs. Dorsay confirmed that Clara was "sensitive and highly strung" and took offence when she was referred to as Black. Perhaps to distance herself from an often hostile society, she decided to make a new life in the United States. Along the way she could alter her own way of living and experiment with fresh ways in a different world which might be more inclined to accept her on her own terms.

After her arrest, there was a bewildering variety of stories of what she had done during the 1880s. The *Telegram* reported that she had gone to Syracuse, New York, where she had started to wear male clothing.[8] Local police suspected that she was a "desperate character" and forced her to move on to Rochester where she again attracted the unwelcome attention of the police. This time she was arrested and "subjected again to an ignominious examination at the hands of a crowd of rough, rude men, acting with the law behind them." Her experiences with the police had hardened her to mistreatment for "Two such experiences would be enough to make a morose, man-hating cynic out of the lightest kind of character." Mrs. Dorsay told reporters that she thought that Clara had stayed in Manitoba for a time. However, the one story that was repeated by several of her acquaintances, and seems to have been closest to the truth, was that she had lived for several years in Chicago. After only a short time there she discovered that single Black women had no prospects of employment outside of being a servant or a "Polk-street" prostitute. Therefore, she passed herself off as a young man and got a job at a livery stable. In this occupation she prospered and eventually became a hack driver. So successful was she at fitting into

Chicago life as a young man that she joined an Episcopalian church and sang in the choir. Trouble began when, during her confirmation classes, a former Toronto resident recognized her and told the Reverend that the young man in his class was really a female in disguise. When confronted with this charge, she did not apologize for the ruse but told the minister that she was compelled to do it, and in any event felt more comfortable living as a man. According to the *World*, "Her experience in Chicago was no doubt a precedent for the donning of the trousers in this city."9

Nevertheless, this unmasking was the end of her Chicago career and, in any case, she had received word that Mrs. McKay was unwell and unable to look after herself. Clara returned to the Queen City.

It was upon her return, probably sometime around 1888, that she and Mrs. McKay moved into the shanty next to the Salvation Army Industrial Home for Young Women. Added to their entourage was Florence and an even younger, white girl, Annie. The mystery behind Flora's origins was something Clara never divulged and perhaps her reluctance to speak was an admission that Flora was her illegitimate daughter. If so, Flora would have been born when Clara was 18 or 19. Mrs. Dorsay was convinced that Flora was Clara's child and attributed Clara's remorseless hostility towards men to this illegitimate birth. While she lived in south Parkdale, Clara undoubtedly got to know the locals including the Clarks and the Westwoods. When Gus Clark left for the Northwest late in 1889, his widowed mother was left without a man to protect the household.10 They invited Clara to stay with them for Mrs. Clark appreciated an armed and defiant woman such as Clara to defend the premises. She declared that "Clara was as good as a man in the house when she was about." However, she soon proved a little too defiant for the Clarks and was asked to leave.

A telling incident occurred a short time thereafter when Clara appeared unannounced on the Clark verandah, marched into the living room and declared that one of the Westwood boys had said something horribly derogatory about Miss Clark. All those present disbelieved it, but Clara was insistent and a companion went to fetch Frank's brother Herbert. He heard her out as she stated that it was Frank Westwood who had made the ungentlemanly remark. Frank was called for. He confronted Clara and gave her a "straight denial." She was advised to leave the Clark's house forthwith as her presence was unwelcome. As Gus Clark recalled, "Clara seemed very much incensed at Frank." While this incident had occurred some four years before the murder, it did show that the parties knew each other and that there was a basis for bad blood between Clara and Frank Westwood.

While the bare facts of the case were laid out by the press, the public was eager to know more about Clara Ford as a person and, in some ways, as a celebrity. What was known was that after she left Parkdale there was a series of moves with Clara taking care of an increasingly feeble Mrs. McKay. Finally, the old lady had to be committed to the inauspiciously named Home for Incurables where she died in April 1894. The little ménage was dispersed with Flora being hired out as a servant for the Phyle family and Clara moving to York Street.

As did many members of Toronto's small Black community, Clara had occasionally worked in hotels. It was known that in July 1893, she had been a kitchen girl in the Gladstone House on Queen Street. The other girls "were suspicious of her sex, and whispered to one another that the new girl, in her appearance and actions, was very much like a man." Even in her moments of leisure, "she would many times throw herself into a pugilistic attitude of defence, at the same time expressing her wish that she had been born a man." One of her friends at the Gladstone reported that Clara had once got a letter from Chicago, and Clara had confided to her that it was from her husband, a white man, who still lived in that city, and by whom she had borne two children. Previously, in the winter of 1893, she had worked as a carver at the Palmer House. This employment came to a dramatic end in February as "She was of a very violent temper and the other girls there were afraid of her, as on one occasion she pulled out her revolver and threatened to shoot one of the waiters. Mrs. Palmer disarmed her and forthwith dispensed with her services."[11] The *Mail* conducted a survey of Parkdale residents who recalled Clara. One remembered that he had once seen her on a streetcar when she had become the brunt of derogatory remarks from some young men. When the car stopped, she got off with them and with no hesitation struck the ringleader. "She was of a fierce temperament," it was stated, "She had an ungovernable temper, and [was] liable to the most dangerous ebullitions of fury."[12]

The *World* published the recollections of Benjamin Vise who had employed Clara in his tailor shop in the summer of 1889.[13] He recalled one occasion when he had knocked down her coat and it landed with a hard metallic thud on the floor. Curious, he examined the coat and was shocked to find a revolver in the pocket. When he confronted her with the weapon, she explained that "when I was on the other side [the United States] I was persistently followed by a man who annoyed me until I killed him." Vise was shocked, especially when she went on to relate how she intended to "do up" a man over a 50 cent debt. Vise sacked her immediately as she "was no doubt of a vicious disposition."

Yet others felt that there was much good in her character. Another Parkdale resident considered Clara to be a clever and industrious person who had tenderly looked after her foster mother. Still, there was a persistent feeling of victimization that followed in her wake for even this lady recalled that Clara often "complained to her that people seemed so much against her."[14] The tailor Samuel Barnett was especially sorry to lose her for she was a fine sewer and earned a premium for her work. Moreover, she was content to work till nine or ten at night and had not taken a holiday during her time with him. He also noted that she kept pretty much to herself and was only visited by little Flora. Barnett could work alone with her for a whole day and not exchange more than half a dozen words.[15] Many of her jobs had been in tailoring where she was remembered as a productive employee, but one who would stand up for her rights. In 1890, she had worked for one Jacob Breslan, and when it seemed that he would not pay back-wages she confronted him and "showed temper" enough to convince Breslan to pay her what was owed.

Chloe Dorsay spoke glowingly of Clara that "her character was above reproach, she never stayed out late at nights and was very hard-working and industrious."[16] Still, Mrs. Dorsay also recalled that Clara was a bundle of anomalies, "a man-hater and was never seen in company with men. She had been known to resent the advances of men made to her on the street in no gentle manner." She always carried her revolver and "was very masculine, and frequently went out in male attire, often wearing a pair of men's pants under her dress." To a *Mail* reporter, Gus Clark confirmed that he had known Clara Ford well and that "she used to dress up in man's clothing, and she had not one revolver, but two, one of which, I remember, was pearl-mounted."[17] It was because of her propensity to dress in men's clothes that Clark had become suspicious of her. He had confided his suspicions to his brother-in-law, but thought it better to say nothing to the police until the inquest was closed.

It was this fondness for male attire that most piqued the public's curiosity. Since her Chicago stay Clara had often resorted to male attire and it was said that "Her masculine manner could not be hidden by petticoats, and she was frequently seen on the streets wearing a stand-up collar and white shirt and disporting herself very much as the advanced woman." Clara Ford wore men's clothing, not as a disguise, but because she preferred it. Stories of her American sojourn had proven that when she had the chance, she had opted to live and dress as a man. This conduct raised issues over the role of

The feminine ideal. Left, The summer costume, Windsor Evening Record, *May 15, 1897; right, Summer dress,* Windsor Evening Record, *May 22, 1897.*

fashion in separating and defining the sexes. If men could wear suits that provided ease of movement, women were at an opposite extreme where they were expected to wear clothing that not only discouraged activity but which could be cruelly uncomfortable to wear even when they were perfectly stationary.[18] Victorian fashion required the female body to be completely covered up, yet at the same time to be sexually arousing. This was effected by burying the figure in fabric and then using whalebone stays that pinched the waist as tightly as possible (and usually displaced organs) and a corset which thrust up and exaggerated the size of the breasts. The addition of bustles accentuated the size of the buttocks, but made any limber activity next to impossible. As painful and confining as these clothes could be, they set women apart by accentuating the female's hips and bust. In the opinion of Thorstein Veblen, the American social critic, "The high heel, the skirt, the impractable bonnet, the corset and the general disregard of the wearer's comfort" were all necessary to prove that "the woman is still, in theory, the economic dependent of the man."

Clara Ford was by no means alone in rejecting the dictates of fashion. American feminist and free-love advocate Tennessee Claflin wore men's clothes in the 1870s.[19] When she permitted a reporter to observe her in a man's banking suit with trousers that were a good three inches above the ankle, he solemnly warned her that "If you wear that out on the streets, there'll be a riot worse than the draft riot." As the century wore on, more women were wearing long pantaloons such as bloomers in their leisure time. The "reform costume" of a calf-length skirt over loose trousers was introduced in the 1850s but interest in it had waned. However, by the 1890s, the bloomer returned (without the short skirt) as a practical garment for the active woman. Bloomers allowed for more freedom of movement to the extent that College Street in Toronto regularly witnessed crowds of bicycling young women who audaciously wore these pantaloons to enable them to ride in safety. By 1894 the

Vic Steinberg, female reporter, prepares to cover a story in male attire. "I stood before my mirror togged out in a man's suit," Toronto News, *Nov. 19, 1894.*

Telegram featured an article on this phenomenon under the menacing title "Is Bicycling Modest?"[20] It noted that these ladies rarely slowed for masculine inspection, but it was feared that split skirts or even knickerbockers on women were not far off. Not only did bloomer-clad bicyclists scandalize the pillars of decent society, the *Dominion Medical Monthly* worried that it was leading to the "blazing saddles" phenomenon, that "Bicycle riding produces in the female a distinct orgasm."[21]

In many of her accounts, Clara described her love of reading books by the lakeside. She was a "devourer of novels," according to the *World,* whose few meagre possessions included several volumes. One of the most popular writers of the day, and one she must undoubtedly have read, was Arthur Conan Doyle. In one of his Sherlock Holmes stories, *A Scandal in Bohemia* (published in 1891), a female singer, Irene Adler, gets the better of Holmes when she masquerades as a young man. Tales such as this, with young women seeking adventure as men, were common in the popular press. "Vic" Steinberg, a female reporter for the *News* frequently disguised herself as a man to give a women's perspective on the secret world of the male. One time, she dressed up as a "young sport" to invade one of the city's holiest of male holies, a cheap saloon.[22] On another, she dressed up as one of the boys to attend a baseball game. Yet it was while she was in conventional female garb she once spied a young fellow admiring "his" new suit and then "gaze ruefully at a heap of feminine apparel." Steinberg noticed the same person reappear a few moments later from a dressing area as a "demure maiden" wearing that same feminine attire. The point of the story was that the maiden had clearly preferred her appearance in man's clothing.[23]

As for Clara, her fondness for male attire seems to have gone well beyond any concern for safety or political statement. Rather, it was part of her ambivalent sexual nature, an outward manifestation that, notwithstanding her sex, she favoured the male aspect of her character. Her mannish traits went beyond mere dress for "the discovery in her room (as part of the police investigation) of a complete shaving kit has lent considerable probability to the statement that she even shaves." Streetcar men knew her as a commuter who was notorious for "the mannish way in which she swung on and off streetcars without waiting for them to stop." The *Mail* felt that its readers would be surprised to learn that their city contained such a "remarkable specimen of humanity, a woman who shaved, smoked, wore men's apparel... read books on love and murder"... and "Today she sits perched upon a throne of notoriety, discussed by thousands of tongues."[24]

As reporters dug deeper into Clara's past, a new motive for the killing emerged. A short time before the incident, a Parkdale newspaper had carried an article making fun of an unnamed lady who paraded through the neighbourhood streets in man's clothing. This

An Ontario woman and her bicycle in the 1890s. Courtesy of the Archives of Ontario, C-7-2-0-1-109.

report was echoed in the Toronto *Telegram*, which carried a story of the "masquerading woman in Parkdale."[25] While Clara was not specifically named, all of Toronto was on the look out for this peculiar person. The description in the newspapers certainly fit Clara and Gus Clark recalled, "she accused young Westwood of giving her away, and was very indignant over the affair." The *World* considered her motives and thought, "she shot down young Westwood simply because of some remark he had made to her respecting her appearance."[26] As she was portrayed in these reports, it seemed that an individual as sensitive to any slight such as Clara Ford might well use violence to seek revenge for her public humiliation.

What really set tongues wagging was the inflammatory description of Clara in the *World*. The newspaper spent two editions describing her unusual character and inferring that she was a serious public menace. The *World* informed its readers that she was, "a sufferer from what the medical authorities call homo-sexuality in other words that she was suffering from what is called sexual perversion."[27] It went on to advise that medical authorities cited numerous cases in which women insisted on wearing men's clothing. She was, the *World* concluded, sexually perverted because, "Physically she is a woman, but on the mental side she has all the characteristics of a man, and this is organically manifested in the shape and size of her feet and hands." This condition also manifested a desire to eschew female occupations and perform other edifying aspects of the male condition. The *World* reported that Clara "smoked, she chewed, she drank, she swore, she spit, she shaved and kept a razor and carried it." The newspaper dwelt on the psychological aspects of her condition, that it was similar to the startling new concepts of "sadism" or "the crimes of cruelty and love – taken in many forms, monstrous and incredible," as described by Dr. Richard von Krafft-Ebing of Vienna. In his 1886 book *Psychopathia Sexualis*, Krafft-Ebing had described these conditions and postulated that women were naturally inclined

Women flirt with change, Toronto News, April 8, 1895.

towards masochism for nature gave women "an instinctive inclination to subordinate to man."[28] Any female such as Clara Ford who
acted in a dominant and aggressive role was therefore acting in a
most perverted manner. Moreover, he concluded that women who
were inclined to cross-dressing were obviously homosexuals for this
condition "may nearly always be suspected in females wearing their
hair short, or who dress in the fashion of men." The *World* described
how those who suffered from this "perverted condition" also manifested an intense sense of rage and jealousy. If young Westwood had
interfered with her in any of her masquerades, "it would be an inter-
ference with what she considered one of her dearest pleasures."
Therefore, any hint that Frank Westwood was culpable were ground-
less, for the true explanation of the murder was that "Frank Westwood
was cut off in his youthful prime by a sexually perverted girl."

If Clara Ford was only a fraction of the demented mad woman
she was portrayed to be in the pages of the *World*, then an obvious

legal recourse would be the insanity defence. English law had long recognized that those not mentally responsible for their acts could not be held criminally responsible. The definition of criminal insanity came from the M'Naghton case of 1843 where a deluded assassin had shot British Prime Minister Robert Peel's secretary. The House of Lords developed a set of rules that if a person was afflicted with an insane delusion so as not to know the nature of what they were doing, or if they did not know what they were doing was wrong, then they could be acquitted on the basis of insanity. While this may have satisfied judges and lawyers, the primitive state of medical understanding of human impulses in the late 19th century made the determination of insanity a very hit and miss affair.

In a case that was contemporaneous to Clara Ford's, Amedee Chatelle of Quebec was charged and convicted of the murder of a little girl in Stratford, Ontario.[29] In a lead editorial entitled "Perverted Nature," the *World* linked the two cases for it noted that Chatelle was a transvestite who displayed a weakness for women's corsets and underwear. His trial in October 1894 showed that when he was arrested he was wearing women's clothes and that since the age of 13 "he had been a slave to an impulse to steal women's linen." His crime was a horrible example of the newly identified phenomenon of sadism that "lust and cruelty frequently occur together." According to the *World*, the personalities and crimes of Clara Ford and Amedee Chatelle were similar "and the murder of young Westwood by Clara Ford also seems to have been similarly perverted." Yet, there was also a warning to Clara's lawyers in the Chatelle case. Even before the crime, he had been an inmate of a mental institution, and at his trial he appeared to be completely delusional, refused all legal counsel and only mumbled in his defence that "Of such is the kingdom of heaven." He was convicted and hanged despite affidavits from several prominent medical authorities that he was insane. In light of this it appeared unlikely that the insanity defence could be the salvation for a far more rational individual such as Clara Ford.[30]

However overblown the press coverage, the Clara Ford case offered the Canadian public a chance to seriously consider issues of uncontrollable human impulses of love and cruelty. Americans had already been looking at such issues since the bizarre Tennessee case of Alice Mitchell.[31] Only two years before the Westwood tragedy, Alice Mitchell had murdered her lesbian lover, Freda Ward. Mitchell had hoped to elope and when Ward had refused, Mitchell slashed her to death with a razor. At the time of her arrest, Alice Mitchell still had some of her victim's blood on her wrist. "Don't wipe it off!" she had pleaded, "It's Freda's blood. I love her so." Mitchell was to all appearances a normal woman except for her "sexual instinct."

Now Canadians could judge for themselves a case with many of the same baffling and disturbing aspects and featuring one of the most liberated eccentrics ever to appear in a Canadian courtroom. As the *World* concluded, "Whether the Westwood tragedy will afford us another example of perverted nature it is too early yet to determine, but the eccentricities of the murderess, if such she be, are so marked as to arouse the suspicion that this case should not be judged by ordinary standards."[32]

CHAPTER SEVEN

The Sweatbox

Perhaps it was not surprising, considering her varied career that Clara Ford adjusted well to jail life. She was eating properly, better than she had while she was living on a seamstress's wage, and receiving visits from friends and supporters including Flora McKay. It was reported that "Clara's dusky face looks fuller and brighter than on the evening of her committal, the lines of care that so strongly marked her face while listening to the damaging evidence of her young daughter, having disappeared."[1] Together with fellow inmates she scrubbed floors and painted cells to make the dingy surroundings a little cheerier. This was just as well, for she would spend half a year in custody awaiting trial.

While she grew acquainted with her new surroundings and companions, the newspapers never ceased to speculate about her case. They were feeding a growing public debate over just what had happened at police headquarters on the evening of November 20.

Clara Ford had been the subject of the "dark art" of interrogation. While neither Slemin nor Reburn had used or even threatened to use force on her, they had applied subtle measures to make her talk. Without using abuse or pain, they had extracted her confession by employing classic interrogation techniques. For starters, they had kept her talking. Clara Ford was not the silent type and around a potential audience she seemed able and eager to talk at length. Even when confronted with an unfamiliar version of her world at the detectives' department, she maintained her haughty demeanour and willingly gave a statement in which she detailed her alibi and maintained her innocence. With this statement in hand, Reburn had called in Flora McKay whose account thoroughly undermined Clara's carefully arranged alibi. This shook Clara but did not cause her to abandon her story. Still, this setback caused her to suggest to the detectives that her friend Mary Crozier could revive the alibi. Until that moment, the detectives were unaware of Crozier or of how her evidence might fit into the whole. Unfortunately for Clara it only made matters worse for it destroyed what little credibility remained to her story of going to see *The Black Crook*, and instead had her headed to Parkdale with a revolver at nine o'clock – plenty of time to get there and commit the murder.

A person as proud as Clara Ford was constitutionally unable to sit in a room surrounded by formidable white men and repeat a lie that was clearly no longer believable. If anything had emerged from her background, it was that she was a proud, fierce woman who would prefer risking death to public humiliation. Reburn's interrogation, which lasted almost seven hours, also served the function of setting Clara Ford apart from friends and workmates who might have offered moral support. In this way the police interrogation, both then and now, is "a vital stage in the process of setting the suspect apart from the rest of conforming society..."[2] The only way back is to co-operate. Besides, as a veteran police investigator once observed, "The

A caricature of Sergeant Reburn, Sergeant of Detectives, as printed in the News, Toronto News, *Nov. 29, 1894.*

truth is... everybody down deep *wants* to tell his or her story... If they feel guilty, they want to get it off their chest. If they feel justified in what they did, they want to explain themselves."[3]

Henry Reburn was perceptive enough to play to this feeling of victimization. He listened sympathetically to her account of how Frank Westwood had molested her and asked why she had not called the police. She shrugged and said that they would have done nothing to help her. Then Clara turned to Reburn and reminded him that if he had a sister who had suffered such an insult, that he would have done the same thing. Reburn played to this feeling and added that if she had acted promptly she would have been justified. In this battle of wits the tables seemed to have been turned to make the murderer the victim for her confession became a vindication of her actions. Reburn's method also led to a degree of rapport between interrogator and subject that made it much easier, not only to confess, but to describe in vivid detail how she had travelled to Lakeside Hall, changed her clothes and prepared to exact her revenge.

Despite the confession, there was a burgeoning public sympathy for Clara. Her partisans in the newspapers, notably the *News* and the *Telegram* warned the public to be wary of confessions obtained "under inquisition." The *News* recounted how she had been under constant police questioning for more than six hours and might have said anything to make them stop. Moreover, the other Toronto newspapers seemed to have already convicted and sentenced the poor girl. Where would they find impartial jurors to sit on her case? Even Crown attorney Curry warned the newsmen that, "If I were counsel for the prisoner, I would have them all up for contempt of court."[4]

Not long after she was bound over for trial, there was a perceptible shift in how the public perceived both Clara and the police. Interestingly, some of this swing was attributable to Arthur Conan Doyle. Sherlock Holmes's creator visited Toronto six days after Clara's arrest. "I was very much interested in the account of the affair," he told reporters, "it is a strangely absorbing mystery." Yet, he offered some striking comments on the police tactics. "As to the present prisoner Clara Ford, I cannot offer an opinion, I never met with a case as hers. The system of closeting a prisoner with an officer and cross-examining her for hours savors more of French than English methods of justice."[5] The Toronto *News* published the outraged comments of a lawyer, James Knowles, who asked why the detectives were allowed, "without a warrant, or even with a warrant, to take possession of an ignorant and helpless female, to establish an inquisition, and for hours, with nobody to aid or advise her, to subject their victim to a system of sweating and cross-examination."[6] Moreover, Knowles stated that his sources within the police department had assured him that Inspector Stark had decided that no lawyer would be allowed to talk with her until the detectives had what they wanted. "Is this just?" Knowles asked. "Several of our judges have emphatically disapproved of any questioning on the part of the detectives whatever." Knowles' view of the law did coincide with that of several

English judges, particularly Justice Cave who felt that any answers to questions by the police ought not to be taken into evidence. However, the state of the law was in flux and the role of the police in interrogating suspects was very much in question. Knowles' analysis conveniently omitted the leading Canadian precedent set in the unfortunate case of Albert Hoyt Day.[7]

On a summer's day in 1890, Day had taken his wife Desiré and a sister to visit an isolated spot overlooking Niagara Falls. Unbeknownst to his wife, Day had recently entered into a bigamist marriage with a young woman in New York. While Day's sister got a drink, he pushed Desiré over the precipice. Upon his sister's return, he confessed to the crime, that he had "shoved her over" the Falls. Under police interrogation, Day gave a number of contradictory stories, one that his wife had been gooseberry picking when she had stumbled accidentally into the cataract; sometime later, he said that they had parted in anger and that he had not seen her again. Much of the prosecution's case hinged on the inconsistent statements given by Day to the detectives after his arrest. Canadian judges were timid creatures, and the trial judge was inclined to apply the English rule: "After a prisoner is in custody the police have no right to ask him questions, and an admission or confession obtained in that way is inadmissible in evidence." Nevertheless, he admitted the statements pending a higher court's ruling. At first, the Court of Appeal seemed sympathetic, for Chief Justice Armour said in an aside, "the practice of cross-examining prisoners [is] reprehensible, and the superiors of the detectives should instruct them not to do so." But the Court concluded that statements to the police, so long as they were not secured by threats or promises of reward and made after the "usual caution," were admissible. Albert Hoyt Day was hanged for his crime.

This rationale was in keeping with the chief English decision of the day in which Lord Coleridge had pronounced that "a confession, in order to be admissible must be free and voluntary" and not extracted by means of threats or promises. To police boosters, such as the Toronto *Star*, Clara's interrogation was consistent with the Day rules. The only question was whether the lead interrogator, Sergeant Reburn, described as "one of the cleverest criminal officers in the country," had stepped over the line. Yet the newspaper noted that at no time had he offered Clara a reward for telling all, neither had he threatened her. "As to the questions asked, it is certain that no innocent person could object to them." Not once, but half a dozen times he had attempted to stop the confession that seemed to be tumbling from the woman's lips. If anything, the police, and especially Reburn, had been partial to Clara, trying to get her to hire a lawyer and plead not guilty to the charge.

Despite the *Star's* view that "there appears to be more sentiment than logic" in the growing feeling that Clara Ford was the victim of a police "sweatbox," there was little doubt that there was a vast public groundswell behind this feeling. One of the newspapers beating the drum the loudest on Clara Ford's behalf was the Toronto *Telegram*. Only hours after her arrest, while details were still scarce, the *Telegram* had taken up the case of Clara Ford with naked enthusiasm.[8] They published her life story with emphasis on her being hounded by the police in New York and subjected to humiliating physical examinations. It was as a result of this that "she seems to have been the victim of persecution which taught her to think herself a sort of outcast from every decent branch of society." The *Telegram* sneeringly dismissed the police account as unlikely if not a flat-out lie. Readers were asked to picture the accused murderess, "a young woman is working industriously in the shop of her employer, where she is known as a hard-working, business-like, lady-like employee." Two detectives snatch her from this friendly environment and proceed to "ransack her room, dive into her trunks and then give her to understand that she is wanted for some crime." Removed to the police station, she is shuttled around from office to

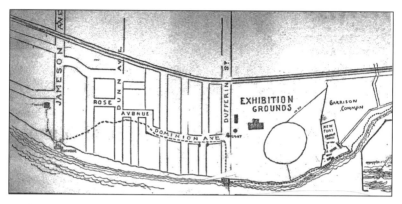

A sketch of the waterfront from Jameson Avenue to Bathurst Street, showing Clara Ford's route, as published in the Telegram, *Toronto* Telegram, *Dec. 1, 1894.*

office. "No chance is given her to get any advice. Six hours she is kept under examination, first by one man then by another... Six hours of detention in the detective department, six hours of quiz and question." Six hours of such gruelling questioning "would drive a strong man to say almost anything. What a woman would say under such circumstances is hard to tell."

While the first argument of Clara's partisans would always be that she was the target of a police sweatbox, it also had to be shown (or at least alleged) that she did not actually kill Frank Westwood. On this point, the *Telegram* was pleased to take its readers through a careful dissection of the police case to show that the confession was so improbable that it had to be untrue. Admittedly, Clara's description of the path taken to Lakeside Hall was entirely possible. There were holes by Dufferin Street where she could have hidden her dress. From there, it would have been simple to proceed down Dominion to Jameson. The gap in the picket fence that she had used to enter the Westwood property was readily visible. However, it was her line of flight that appeared to be improbable. For its readers' use, the *Telegram* published a detailed map of the crime scene and route.

Returning to Dufferin Avenue and putting on her skirt and jacket, Clara had proceeded to the wharf at the foot of Dufferin. According to the police, Clara had told them that she had walked under the wharf and from there along the waterfront, across by the New Fort, and through the Old Fort to the foot of Bathurst Street. From there, she had walked north back to the Dorsay boarding house.

There was a great deal that was wrong about this, and it all had to do with the New Fort, a military structure to the east of the Exhibition Grounds. The western fence was twelve feet high and, if Clara had to go around this fence, she would have had to traverse a barely submerged pile of rocks. As an athletic *Telegram* reporter attested, this was difficult and dangerous during the day for "anyone passing would be obliged to wade out around these stones." At night it would have been all but impossible. Furthermore, on the night of October 6, the lake level had been a foot higher "and it may be classed as an impossibility for her to have done it." Impossibility? As an afterthought, the report noted that there was a spot in the fence where two pickets were missing and anyone who "knows the ropes" could have used this breach to avoid the water and simply cross the garrison grounds. Moreover, Reburn had not said that she had exclusively used the waterfront, instead he had repeated her comments to him that she had gone, "across to the old fort." Despite this, the *Telegram* was confident that the story as related by the police had now been exposed as a fraud.

Sympathy for Clara was spreading beyond Toronto. The Ottawa *Free Press* noted that the only evidence against her was the statement to the police and, "Whether this very improper course will be endorsed by the Court remains to be seen."9 In Quebec, the Montreal *Gazette* also questioned the police methods. They felt that these interrogation techniques belonged to the French inquisitorial system rather than to the refined notions of English law. It was unlikely, the *Gazette* felt, that such a confession would be allowed in an English court for

"It is entirely contrary to the spirit and practice of English law to cross-question the accused and confront her with the witness she says can prove her alibi." The Toronto *Telegram* heartily endorsed this view for in its opinion, "The French practice of badgering the accused and practising every act and subterfuge in order to obtain an admission of guilt" worked admirably to secure convictions but could just as easily lead to the conviction of the innocent.

The Toronto police had also subjected men to gruelling interrogations, but this had not attracted the same level of public concern. What brought Clara Ford's case to the fore was that she was a woman and, above all, a woman who was defending her honour. She had been "insulted" (usually a euphemism for rape or attempted rape) by Frank Westwood and, as she had insisted to the police, her race and class precluded her having access to the law. In a study of rape prosecutions in York County, it appeared that men of high status were almost always believed and were rarely charged with rape. And as for the victims, "only credible women were deemed worthy of protection." Therefore, vigilantism was Clara's only recourse. This may have been a case where she sought, as Carolyn Strange phrased it, "tacit approval" to mete out justice to a man who had robbed her of her dignity, for in the defence of honour, it was permissible "for women to kill villains whom men routinely exculpated."[10] A lady defending her virtue was a potent defence in Victorian Canada. The difficulty lay in the inability of a mercurial character such as Clara Ford to fit the model of the proper Victorian lady.

Catharine Beecher's 1841 discourse, *Treatise on Domestic Economy*, had defined the role of women to succeeding generations. She was supposed to crush all desire and personal ambition and devote herself exclusively to home and husband. Within this proper sphere, keeping house and educating daughters should occupy all of a middle-class matron's attentions. As Barbara Welter portrayed her in her seminal article "The Cult of True Womanhood, 1820-1860," the "true woman" of Victorian times displayed these cardinal virtues: "Piety, purity, submissiveness and domesticity. Put them all together and they spelled mother, daughter, sister, wife – woman."[11] None of the above seemed to apply to a revolver-toting, pants-wearing individual such as Clara Ford. Any lady who leaped off of moving streetcars and who challenged anyone, Black or white, man or woman who defied her, was about as far from the Victorian ideal as it was possible to get.

Until about 1880, most single women in Toronto had worked in domestic service.[12] However, in the following decades there was a huge influx of young women into the industrial workforce. For example, Christie Brown bakeries expanded rapidly during the 1880s, and most of its workers or "jam-dollopers" were female. Still, most Toronto women worked in the city's garment or shoe industries. Clara was one of the former, an employee in a small, semi-permanent dress shop. Like most single working women, her job was marginal, dependent upon the seasons or fashion, paid very little and might only last for a few months. As a single, working woman she did not conform to the prevailing standards for domesticity and submissiveness. Moreover her unusual lifestyle precluded her from being considered the middle-class ideal of the pure woman. Yet, however unconventional her conduct she was still a woman and, in the Canada of the 1890s, this counted for a great deal indeed. For a jury to find that a woman was capable of a violent premeditated attack against a man was a serious affront to deep convictions of femininity that all women were essentially pure and decent creatures.

Women were held in such noble regard even though they were among Victorian society's foremost killers. The difference was that their crimes were ones of desperation and their victims were invariably their newborn children. The poverty and shame resulting from a birth out of wedlock frequently compelled women to commit infanticide.[13] The overwhelming disgrace of an illegitimate birth was likely the reason that Clara never acknowledged or discussed Flora's origins. Small bodies found in privies or alleys were a sad but common feature of 19th century life. Yet, it may have been a good omen for Clara's defenders that male judges and juries tended to take a lenient attitude, even towards women who had murdered children, for "most judges and juries refused to convict the female perpetrators of infanticide, even in cases of gruesome and indisputable evidence." To that extent, violence by mothers against their children seems to have been accepted as the custom of the country.

Another potent argument in the arsenal of her defence was that of race. Belonging to the most marginal group in society could be turned to her advantage; already the *World* had suggested that her racial background required that she be judged by a different standard. The newspaper recounted her mean beginnings that she had been a pariah at school and "As she grew older she realized that it was to the presence of African blood in her veins that many of the buffs she had received were due. She brooded on this fact, and the untold, untellable suffering and misery which people of her colour had suffered in the past."14 It even suggested that Blacks were essentially different from whites; that is, her racial background also left her at the mercy of an uncontrollable inclination, a "wild impulse" to strike out at any insult. In 19th century Ontario, Blacks were thought to be "lazy, improvident, docile... this placid exterior, however, masked a passionate fury buried deep within the Black character that might burst forth unpredictably in a frenzied orgy of destruction..."15 Perhaps it should be taken into account that Clara's actions were only the result of her unfortunate racial instincts. All of these factors, her victimization in the "sweatbox," her status as a single female in a hostile world, the disability of her race, were all a potent mixture that, in the hands of manipulative defence counsel, might win her back her life.

To that end, her original lawyer, W.G. Murdoch, had sought out the help of another lawyer to assist with Clara's defence. Clara's new lead counsel was perhaps the best defence lawyer in the country. Ebenezer Forsyth Blackie Johnston was Scottish by birth and had risen quickly in public life.[16] He had become the province's deputy attorney-general from 1885 to 1890. Thereafter, he had concentrated on the courtroom and was renowned as a great cross-examiner, that rare breed of verbal fencer who can take an otherwise straight forward story and look at it from so many different angles that the jurors would not think it very straight forward at all. He was reputed to take such a cold, logical approach that, "When defending a case, he declined as a rule to see his client, but merely asked that he should be placed in possession of the facts; and then he sat down, like a mathematician solving a problem, to work out the best possible line of defence." Blackie Johnston handled both prosecutions and defences and ironically had conducted the Crown prosecution of Albert Day in 1890. On that occasion, he had successfully defended the conduct of the detectives whose grilling of the suspect rivalled that in the Ford case. In his summation at the Day trial, he had spoken "very highly of the detectives and the fairness and moderation with which they had treated the prisoner."

Why would Johnston take on the case of a client who could never pay? Perhaps because the Ford trial would be widely reported and would make an ideal stage for his talents. Besides, she had already confessed and if she were convicted he would not be blamed. If she was acquitted, the public would consider it little short of a miracle and a lawyer who could work miracles could attract legions of paying clients. Johnston and Murdoch also had to contend with recent changes in the law that had drastically altered the way criminal trials were conducted. One legacy of Sir John A. Macdonald's nation building was the enactment of a national Criminal Code in 1892. Unlike Britain, whose criminal law was still found in a bewildering variety of statutes and judicial decisions, or the United States where each state created its own codes, Canada had one Criminal

Code that regulated the lives of its citizens. The Criminal Code would impact on the Clara Ford trial in subtle, but important ways. For one thing, the rules on the plea of insanity had been codified by section 11. However, due to a draftsman's error, this section required the prisoner to prove that he or she was incapable of appreciating the nature and quality of the act *and* that the act was wrong. The original test only required that one of these standards be met. This made it doubly difficult to rely on an insanity defence and Clara's lawyers opted to forego any reliance on this plea. However, assisting them was a further amendment in 1893, which for the first time permitted accused persons to take the witness stand and tell their side of the story. No doubt, Clara's lawyers relished the prospect of putting their client, the vulnerable, wounded female, into the stand.

As Murdoch and Johnston marshalled their forces for trial, they would attempt to develop those defences already so richly detailed in the pages of the Toronto *Telegram* that the confession was improbable and obtained under duress. Unknown to them, the prosecution was also at work preparing a new theory of the motive; one which would strip Clara Ford of the high moral ground. If the Crown's theory succeeded, she would no longer be seen as a disadvantaged woman protecting her honour, but instead revealed to all as a jealous and conniving murderer.

CHAPTER EIGHT

Revelations of an Improper Sort

The new year of 1895 began in Toronto in fire and death. On January 6, the *Globe* building at Yonge and Melinda burned down, causing a half million dollars in damage and killing a fireman.[1] A week later, an even larger fire consumed the Osgoodby Building and several adjoining warehouses and offices.[2] One woman was trapped in the building and jumped to what appeared to be her death only to be saved by a labyrinth of telegraph wires that cushioned her fall. Toronto firemen had woefully inadequate equipment that could barely throw water as high as four storeys, and were able to do little to stop the conflagrations. One of the reporters on the grim scenes was the *News* intrepid girl reporter, Vic Steinberg. Another newsman climbed to the top of the Canada Life building and described the Osgoodby Building fire as, "one of inspiring grandeur. At every second the detail of the scene changed, as with the turning of a kaleidoscope, but ever the same blood-red colour of the awful element covered the whole picture."

A Toronto News *sketch depicting the fall of the front of the Osgoodby Building in the "Great Fire" of January 1895, Toronto* News, *Jan. 11, 1895. The building, located on Melinda Street just east of Bay, was described as one of "the finest warehouses in the city,"* Globe, *Jan. 11, 1895.*

Shortly after noon on Saturday, January 19, 1895, when much of Toronto's western business district was still smoldering, the case of Clara Ford was called before a grand jury to determine if a "true bill" authorizing the trial to proceed should be issued. There was a sudden rush to the courthouse to catch the results. The Clerk of the Court rose and read the grand jury's verdict "Queen v. Clara Ford. True Bill. Murder."[3] Clara was immediately arraigned and pleaded not guilty.[4] This was no real surprise, given the weight of the evidence that the case would go on to trial. The question was when. In the normal course, her trial would have come on in the March assizes. However, W.G. Murdoch asked for a postponement to the spring for he advised the Court that the defence was trying to find additional witnesses who would attest to Clara's whereabouts on the night of the murder. As well, he filed affidavits to the effect that public opinion was so poisoned against her that it would be difficult to get a fair trial. He failed to explain how a delay would alleviate this situation. Mr. Justice William Street, not known as a patient judge, dismissed Murdoch's motion and ordered that a trial date be set the following week.

The next Monday, Blackie Johnston took another attempt at an adjournment. If they only had more time, he argued, the defence would be able to show that Clara did have an alibi. The prosecution had more than thirty witnesses and "as the case is one of unusual magnitude and gravity, and as it will turn upon many fine points and questions of fact, he should have adequate time to prepare."[5] As delicately as he could, Justice Hugh MacMahon expressed his view that Street may have been a little hasty and granted the postponement. The case was put over to the assizes of April 30, to be heard before Chancellor Boyd.

On that day, the cab bearing Clara Ford and two constables pulled up in front of the Adelaide Street courthouse.[6] In the intervening six months, the public had lost none of its interest in the Westwood tragedy for long before the appointed hour, crowds had been gathering around the (as the *Globe* called it), "ramshackle old courthouse." Noted for its dingy white brick walls surmounted by a plain dome, the Adelaide Street courthouse had been marked ten years before this trial to, "be replaced by something less unworthy of the capital of Ontario." But it was not, and the old building soldiered on. At the request of the press, the sheriff had installed additional desks for reporters to record the proceedings. In addition to the newsmen, the growing crowd of onlookers spilled out into the corridors and milled around the grounds. At first, the sheriff only admitted witnesses, jurors and the lawyers as it was apparent that the old courthouse could not handle the crush of spectators.

After the grand jury was empanelled, the case of Regina v. Clara Ford was called and Clara, flanked by the two constables, walked briskly up the aisle and into the iron prisoner's dock. To the reporters she remained "the young mulatto girl whose strange career and still stranger confession" had captivated the city the previous fall. Before

Clara Ford at the time of her arraignment, Toronto News, *Nov. 28, 1894.*

CLARA FORD.
(DRAWN FROM LIFE)

sitting down she turned and looked around the courtroom as if searching for someone, though apparently without success.

As usual she displayed no trace of anxiety. Journalists noted that she wore the same black cloth jacket with beaver edging that she had worn at the preliminary hearing. It is most likely that she owned nothing else. Jail life had agreed with her to the extent that she had put on weight since she was last in the public eye. There was little time wasted in selecting the jury (one of whom Clara personally objected to) of respectable white tradesmen and mechanics from Toronto or the townships around the city.

Presiding over the affair would be the province's Chancellor, John Alexander Boyd.7 A tall, patrician figure, his face framed by a conventional set of mutton-chop whiskers, Boyd had already served as a judge for fourteen years. His specialty was chancery, that part of the law dealing with mortgages and estates. In fact, Boyd was Ontario's last Chancellor appointed before the jurisdictions of equity and common law were joined. Not only was he a formidable being in appearance, he was also a leader of the Baptist Church, an officer of McMaster University and a man who, even in his family circle, referred to himself as "The Chancellor."

However, if there was one celebrity in the courtroom, one who almost overshadowed Clara Ford herself, it was the Crown prosecutor, Britton Bath Osler. Osler cut an imposing figure in any courtroom. Just shy of six feet, he was thickset with a bald head offset by an enormous walrus mustache. In 1874, a gas explosion in his house had almost killed his wife and himself. Many knew the story of how Osler had re-entered the burning house to save a maidservant by carrying her out and rolling her in a carpet to extinguish the flames. The effort had nearly cost him his life for he was described as, "his head, face and hands having been literally roasted."[8] He was left with fearsome scars on his hands and neck and never regained full use of his limbs. This disfigurement in no way set back his legal career for Osler came from exceptional stock. One brother, Featherstone, became a judge while a younger brother, Edmund, became a leading financier and politician. The pride of the Oslers, the youngest son William, became a distinguished medical teacher in both America and Europe. As for Britton Osler, he had become the foremost trial lawyer of his day, the man the government turned to whenever a case absolutely had to be won. In 1885, he was called on to prosecute Louis Riel and after that to handle a multi-million dollar arbitration with the Canadian Pacific Railway. Only a few weeks before the Clara Ford trial, he had acted on behalf of Toronto's mayor, Warring Kennedy, in warding off a legal challenge to his re-election. Osler was such an effective advocate that opposing counsel complained that whenever he argued a case, his scarred hand clutching the jury rail, he became like the "thirteenth juryman," such a dominant personality that jurors would hesitate to contradict him. Rarely in Canadian law has a lawyer been so regarded as the master of the courtroom.

Osler's presence in the Court was a sign of just how seriously the government took this prosecution. Nor was he alone, for assisting him would be Crown attorneys Hartley Dewart and J.W. Curry. This formidable array of judge and lawyers was an impressive embodiment of wealth and position in Canadian society. Even the jurors, all white and all male, were stolid member of the respectable middle class. They all stood in odd juxtaposition to the prisoner in the dock. Clara Ford, a poor Black woman, could not have travelled farther from her own spectrum of society than to be in the company of the men who were about to try her for her life.

Whoever the prisoner, the Anglo-American world loved a murder. After seven persons were hacked to death in Denham, England, in 1870, "pleasure vans" brought hordes of Londoners to the site of the slaughter to gasp at the scene. Even Denham could not compare to the sensation created by the Whitechapel murders of 1888. Detailed accounts of the slaughter and dissection of London prostitutes by "Jack the Ripper" were delivered to the nation's breakfast tables via the newspapers.[9] The institutionalization of murder as a source of public entertainment owed a good deal to the mass press of the late 1800s. That period saw the emergence of wide circulation newspapers and for the first time, the general public in Britain and America could read of horrid events and their consequences almost at the time they happened. Murder trials made for exceptionally good press and, in Toronto, six major dailies competed for the public's attention and each widely reported the Clara Ford trial.

This was by no means the first time that Canadians had been enthralled by a case of spectacular justice. The public enjoyed the high drama of a murder trial if for no other reason than to read accounts of bloody mayhem in what was now a rather sedate society. The vicarious thrill provided by the Victorian murder was especially apparent when Reginald Birchall, a dapper English gentleman stood accused of killing Fred Benwell in 1890.[10] Birchall had lured Benwell to Woodstock in Oxford County, with the prospect of buying a farm. Once there, Birchall had murdered him, removed all identifying tags from his clothes, and left his corpse in an isolated swamp at nearby Princeton. By chance, his body was soon recovered and Birchall was accused. On the first day of his trial, 1,500 people jammed into the area of the courthouse. Telephone connections suspended over the judge carried the proceedings to another building where banks of telegraph operators sent instantaneous reports of the trial to newspapers across Canada, the United States and Britain. A charming rogue, Birchall chuckled that the colonials had simply gotten the wrong man. However the Crown prosecutor, the same B.B. Osler, presented a meticulously detailed forensic account of how Birchall had carried out the killing. Birchall was convicted and hanged. Significantly, Mrs. Birchall, who must have been equally complicit in the scheme, was not even charged.

When a lady stood accused of murder the public's fascination went up by several degrees of magnitude. Less than two years before Clara's trial, Lizzie Borden of Fall River, Massachusetts, faced trial for the axe murder of her parents. The Borden case created a sensation across the United States and ended with the jury being unable to convict and hang such a pleasant and demure lady. Even though Lizzie's story of having been in a barn while her father and step-mother were slaughtered was implausible and subject to occasional change, and even though she had burned a dress shortly after the murders, it was inconceivable that the proper Miss Borden might be an axe murderer. As one writer observed, "Lizzie Borden owed her life largely to these tacit assumptions: ladies aren't strong enough to swing a two pound hatchet... Ladies cry a lot. Ladies love to stay home all the time. Ladies are ceaselessly grateful to the men-fathers or husbands who support them."[11] It was taken for granted that ladies did not stalk and murder men. Moreover, it might have been a lesson to Clara's defence that femininity appealed to the male juror. In England, Maria Manning, a rough and sexually aggressive woman, was hanged for murder, while Adelaide Bartlett, a gentle and ladylike creature who claimed to have had sexual intercourse only once and that for the purpose of procreation, was acquitted. The evidence against both women had seemed persuasive.[12] The difficulty lay in portraying Clara Ford as a demure, feminine creature, particularly with layers of media coverage emphasizing her tendency to mannish behaviour.

Bizarre murder tales added a frisson to the lives of most working people for although literacy had spread, most people still were compelled to work at numbingly repetitive jobs that offered little excitement. In addition to the newspapers, popular entertainments often dealt with the theme of honour killings. It seemed to be a staple of the musical halls to offer a show where a young woman (frequently disguised in boy's clothing) defended her virtue and had license to take any steps, including murder, to avenge her lost honour.[13] Now what might have been a cheap melodrama was elevated into a dramatic event starring Clara Ford as the aggrieved heroine and presenting details even more salacious than the local theatre dared display. A prosecutor as astute as B.B. Osler realized that one way to get Clara Ford off centre stage was to regain the initiative and change her role to something other than that of the heroine.

Osler's opening address began in a typical workmanlike manner. As an impartial representative of Her Majesty, it was Osler's duty to justly present the evidence and see that there was a fair trial. On his part, there was no urgency to obtain a conviction. The onus was on the Crown, he conceded, to prove guilt beyond a reasonable doubt. Dispassionately, he gave a brief outline of the facts and a description of the tragic scene. The first surprise in his opening, something never disclosed before, was an anomaly in the bullet that linked it to

The Crown prosecutor Britton Bath Osler. Courtesy of the Law Society Archives.

the revolver found in Clara Ford's bedroom. Her pistol was of "cheap German manufacture" but had a peculiar defect in one of the chambers that did not properly align with the barrel. As well, there was a small projection in the barrel, which would leave a striation on the bullet. The bullet extracted from the body of Frank Westwood bore all the marks of having been fired from this specific revolver. The *Globe* noted, "This somewhat startling statement created much interest, and indicates how fully and carefully the Crown case has been prepared."[14]

Osler then moved on to the confession. Admittedly, only the criminal and the victim were present at the scene and the Crown had no direct information on what had occurred. But they did have the confession of November 20. Osler assured the jurors that every warning had been given to Clara Ford before she had given her detailed account of how she had planned and carried out the killing of Frank Westwood. "In this confession, under the circumstances in which it was given – told to more than one and after the crime had been denied – is this one of the class of confessions that has a right to be regarded with suspicion?" he asked. Above all this was the question, why? What had brought these two improbable characters together on the verandah of Lakeside Hall that Saturday night? Osler cautioned that the Crown did not have to prove motive, that if it demonstrated the act, that this alone was sufficient to secure a conviction. Nevertheless, the Crown had discovered a motive and was prepared to share it with the jury.

Frank Westwood and Clara Ford were lovers.

There was, Osler delicately advised the jurors, evidence of a "certain relationship of an improper sort existing between the deceased and this woman."[15] This relationship would be shown through the testimony of a female (admittedly a person of low character) but one who had been familiar with both Clara and Frank. This woman would confirm that Clara had seen Frank with another woman and had furiously warned that woman that if she was seen again with Frank that "there would be a shooting." Far from being a wounded heroine, Clara's notorious temper had been aroused when she saw her young white lover with another woman and as a consequence "jealousy produced this crime."

This latest revelation created a sensation in the courtroom and dramatically altered the roles of the parties. Eighteen-year-old Frank Westwood was perhaps mature beyond his years and more subject to "entanglements" than his friends had previously let on. It also meant that instead of defending herself from insult, Clara was simply a frustrated woman fearful of losing a prize catch to another. The *World*, a newspaper singularly opposed to Clara's cause, described this latest shocker, "Westwood's death is the old story of love and passion, condemned by the law of God and man. It is the story of a mulatto girl, who had been the plaything of an apparently respectable young man. Discarded by him for another, she deliberately shot him down." According to this account, the cloud of shame that hung over Frank was thereby dissipated for he was cleared of any allegations of sexual assault. While Osler insinuated that his conduct was not correct, at least he had the sense to put an end to this relationship "of an improper sort." This latest revelation also addressed a number of unanswered questions left over from the inquest for it "explains the remarks of the young man before his death that 'Mum's the word' and 'You can't pump me' and it gives credence to the opinion generally held at the time of the shooting that Westwood knew who fired the shot." During Osler's address Clara had watched him, although occasionally her eyes wandered to the bank of reporters who were furiously transcribing his words. Would they pay such close attention to her? Outwardly, she preserved the same stolid indifference, as one reporter noted an "almost uninterested demeanour."

There was not much time remaining in the day, so Osler decided to call witnesses who could lay the groundwork for the prosecution's case. Clara Westwood repeated her story of the late night call, the sudden report of a pistol and the cry of 'Mother, I am shot.' " The speculation must have crossed her mind many times what would have happened had she answered the door that night. Frank was a good boy who, she insisted, "had no entanglements." What she thought of the Crown's assertion that her boy was the lover of a Black woman almost twice his age is again only a matter for speculation. While at the inquest, Frank Westwood had been continually lauded as a noble youth, Clara Westwood now had to endure the Crown attorney describing her son's involvement in an unusual relationship. Benjamin Westwood again testified as to his actions on that Saturday night.[16] He recalled that the pickets were off of the fence and that anyone could easily have gained access. The defence had to be circumspect in their cross-examination of the still grieving parents and Murdoch decided to limit himself to only a few questions. Still, these few queries could set the stage for the defence's case. Murdoch asked if he knew Clara Ford. He did not, Westwood replied, but his children did:

Q: Did Frank know her?
A: I expect he did.
Q: Did you ever hear him speak of her?
A: No.

In this simple exchange, the ground was being set for a case that even one of the Crown's witnesses was unsure if Clara and Frank even knew each other.

After Benjamin Westwood stepped down, the prosecution unsheathed what it hoped would be one of its most potent weapons. With a flourish, Osler reached across the prosecution desk and from a small envelope produced a bullet. Dr. Orr who had conducted the inquest identified this as the bullet taken from the body of the deceased. This was, as the *News* called it, the "missile of death" which had claimed Frank's life and "upon this point alone the Crown laid great stress and have forged a complete chain of evidence showing that the revolver which was found in the possession of Clara Ford is the weapon which fired the bullet taken from the body of Frank Westwood."[17]

As the lawyers were handing around the bullet for inspection, Osler became increasingly worried over its treatment. Twice he called the attention of the Court to Blackie Johnston's conduct of continually fingering the bullet and that "there were certain marks upon it which could easily be rendered indecipherable." He need not have worried. Johnston was planning to destroy the bullet evidence in cross-examination, not by any surreptitious mauling.

As the case closed for the day and the opening rituals concluded, it might have appeared to some to be a theatre of the absurd. The prisoner had not only confessed her guilt several times, she had admitted to it in open Court. But the formalities of due process had to be respected and, in any event, the newspaper-reading public expected drama and surprise. In the next four days they would get liberal doses of both.

CHAPTER NINE

The Crown's Case

Mary Crozier, perhaps Clara's best friend in Toronto, stepped hesitantly into the witness box the next morning. Mrs. Crozier had known her for four years and Clara had even lived with the Crozier family for a time. Mary still did Clara's laundry and they had visited each other during off work hours. On the evening of October 6, Clara had been visiting with the Croziers at their house at 24 Camden Street. As she was going to a show with Flora MacKay, Clara explained that she would leave her laundry with Mary and pick it up later. Young Maggie Crozier noticed that Clara had a revolver in her coat pocket. This detail was not too unusual for the Croziers knew that Clara regularly carried a pistol. What was strange was that the usually abstemious Clara had obviously been drinking. Two days later she was again at the Croziers and perusing accounts of the Westwood murder in a newspaper. Mary recalled her peculiar comment that, "I'm glad I wasn't there or I'd be blamed for it. I know that place and lived with a

Clara Ford's friends, Mrs. Mary Crozier (right) and Maggie Crozier,
Toronto News, *May 1, 1895.*

woman near the Westwoods; I often took a book down to the lakeside
to read. It was a good job I was not up there or they would say I did
it."[1] As she mused over the newspaper accounts, Clara remarked that
she had known Frank Westwood since he was a child. She also added
that whoever did the shooting must have known Parkdale well as the
only escape route would have been a circuitous path along the lakefront. It was on this visit that Clara gave Mary's son the fedora she had
been wearing the previous Saturday night.

William Murdoch's cross-examination gained little for the
defence for it only elicited glowing character references from Mary
Crozier for her friend. In Mrs. Crozier's opinion, "I believe anything
she says; she is honest, industrious and has a good character."[2]
Obviously, she was a reluctant Crown witness and this only added to
the ringing veracity of her testimony. But before she left the stand,
Murdoch did extract one useful point. Mary had seen Clara pull up
her skirt to adjust her stockings. To her, it appeared that Clara had
not been wearing any men's clothes underneath her skirt.

The next witness, Maggie Crozier, took spectators and reporters aback. She was a stunningly beautiful girl whose testimony backed up that given by her mother. Maggie had seen Clara in men's clothes on other occasions and she also recalled her surprising comments after the Westwood tragedy. Maggie's sister Sadie was also present and added one original detail. Sadie recalled that Clara had said that she was going to Parkdale to fetch her "daughter" Flora. The Crozier family (all being persons partial to the accused) had established that Clara had not been to see *The Black Crook* on the night of October 6 but rather that she had been drinking, carrying a gun and was on her way to Parkdale at about 9 o'clock that night.

The trial's second day was filled with the prosecution's introduction of a myriad of details that they hoped would lead to a conclusion of guilt. Witnesses from the neighbourhood swore that they heard the fatal shot a few minutes before eleven. Frank's pals, Temple Cooper and Ed Lennox, swore that they had left him at his house shortly after ten and that, "they never knew deceased to have entanglements with women." At this, newspaper reporters noticed, "A contemptuous smile passed over the prisoner's countenance when this portion of the examination was in progress."

While Clara had shown little interest in the Crown's case so far, she straightened and gripped the bar in front of her as the next witness, Flora MacKay, was called to the stand. A *Globe* reporter described her as a, "very nice looking girl with a great wealth of dark hair, and the olive complexion which indicates much southern or a slight tinge of African blood in her veins." She had known Clara "for as long as I can remember." Nor was she a casual friend for Clara had talked with her employer, Mrs. Phyle, and asked her to watch over Flora and make sure that she did not stay out late at night. On Friday, October 5, Clara had arranged to meet her at 7:30 the following evening at the corner of Bay and Queen. Clara had never appeared and Flora had returned home. Nothing further was said about the missed date until the following week when Clara asked Flora if she had heard about the Westwood shooting. Clara suggested that Gus Clark had something to do with it. She also instructed Flora that if Mrs. Phyle or anyone else asked where they were on Saturday, to tell them that they had been together watching *The Black Crook*.

Osler was about to ask her about her visit by the detectives when Johnston rose to protest. In a foreshadowing of his objections on the admissibility of the confession, he argued that Flora's statements to the police were all a part of a tainted process. However, as Flora denied that the detectives had threatened her in any way, Chancellor Boyd instructed Osler to continue:

> Q: What did she [Clara] say?
> A: She said that she told me that she was up at Parkdale on October 6 and for me not to say any-thing about it.[3]

Flora then described her talks with the detectives in which she had, at first, maintained that they had been at the theatre together. After Sergeant Reburn told her "that if she did not tell the truth she would get into trouble" she admitted that Clara had coached her into giving a lie.

Once again, the attempt to cross-examine this unwilling Crown witness only seemed to reinforce her testimony. As far as Clara's comment that she was in Parkdale that night, the little girl insisted, "She never told me she was, but she thought she told me, and told me not to tell." As Murdoch took her through the various stories she had told the police, a few contradictions emerged and as he chal-lenged her on these points the girl began to sob. Finally, as if to resolve the confusion, she exclaimed:

> I was not at the theatre the night Mr. Westwood

was shot. I thought they would think Clara was
guilty if I did not say I was there. I don't think she
is guilty.

At this point, the girl completely dissolved in tears and Chancellor
Boyd called a brief recess. Again the Crown had scored a major
point. The prisoner's putative daughter had unwillingly admitted
that she was trying to cover Clara's tracks on the night of the murder.

Mrs. Phyle confirmed Flora's account for she also remembered
the girl coming home early about eight o'clock. Murdoch vigorously
cross-examined Mrs. Phyle and reduced her to tears as well. But it
was all to no purpose. She insisted that Flora had come home early
and that it was on the night of the Westwood murder. These inter-
locking narratives were beginning to serve their function by creating
a convincing story that led inexorably to Clara's guilt.

It was a sign that the Crown prosecution was getting closer to the
heart of its case when Detective Charles Slemin was called on that
afternoon. He had just begun to describe Clara's arrest when
Johnston objected.[4] He noted that at the time of the "arrest" no caution had been given to the accused. Turning the tables on him,
Chancellor Boyd pointed out that in the case of Albert Day the suspect's comments to the police were admitted and constituted the
evidence upon which he was hanged. Undoubtedly every policeman
and lawyer in the courtroom appreciated the irony that it was
Johnston, who had argued so strenuously and successfully in the
Day case that the interrogation evidence be admitted, who was now
seeking the opposite result. But there was a difference here,
Johnston insisted. In Clara's case Slemin and Porter had never
warned her before she began to talk. Boyd waved off the objection
and Slemin continued to relate how they had picked up Clara and
taken her up to her room. Once there, they had found a suit of
men's clothes and a revolver. When it was apparent that the police

were interested in the revolver, she had exclaimed, "Oh, it's the Westwood case you are after," and hastily explained that while it appeared that the gun had been fired recently that she had been shooting at ducks. She further advised them that she had been to a show that Saturday night and a young friend of hers could attest to this. All of these words had come tumbling from her lips with no prompting from the detectives or before they had even mentioned the name "Westwood."

At this point, Osler asked the detective to describe the experiments that were made with the gun. Slemin explained how a four-pound side of beef about an inch thick had been used and a light cloth similar to a vest placed over it. Then Clara's gun had been fired six times into the beef from a distance of three feet. The description of the test seemed to amuse the spectators and the prisoner for it was reported, "she laughed heartily on more than one occasion."[5] Her lawyers, however, did not find it amusing. Johnston asked why they had selected flesh with no bone. This was not very realistic, was it? When Johnston asked to look at the six test bullets, Osler refused on the grounds that "if the sealed envelopes were opened by others than those who made the experiment, the means of identification would be lost." Johnston then astutely focused his cross-examination on the question of whether or not Clara was under arrest at the time she was apprehended. Slemin crossed verbal swords with him on this point and the detective maintained that while she was not at liberty and was obliged to go with them to headquarters, that she was not technically under arrest and therefore did not have to be warned. But the point had been made, if not to the judge then to the jury, that this was an example of high-handed and perhaps devious conduct on the part of the police.

As the case ground on, the poor ventilation in the courtroom and the crush of bodies began to take its toll. A *Telegram* reporter observed that "the crowd in the room is suffocating" and that many were obliged to stand three hours or more to listen to the testimony.

Many ladies were present and "they don't miss a word of the trial, no matter what is under discussion." As for the prisoner, she "evidently felt the burden of the hot, close and unhealthy atmosphere. She looked worn and tired; the intensity of the trial is, apparently, beginning to take its toll on her nerves."[6]

Her spirits might have brightened considerably if she knew that the Crown's case was on the brink of disaster.

As its last witness on what had already been a long day, Osler called Libby Black to the stand. This was a new name never before linked to the Westwood case and the crowd buzzed in anticipation of some startling revelations. Mrs. Black herself did not appear too promising. A weathered survivor of Toronto's streets, she was described by the *News* as a "debauched-looking female."[7] She readily admitted that she was currently serving a sixty-day sentence (her third) for public drunkenness. Some time before June 1894 she had met Frank Westwood on Spencer Avenue in Parkdale. They talked for a few minutes until he crossed the street and met a woman Mrs. Black identified as Clara Ford. A few days later Frank again talked to her at the corner of Massey and King streets. After they parted, Clara Ford accosted her and warned, "You had not better talk to him any more or I will do for you." From these two chance meetings it was inferred that Clara and Frank were lovers and that Clara would kill any rival who sought his affections.

As surprisingly slight as this was, it was the full extent of the Crown's case on the illicit relationship. Yet it sent a shock wave through the courtroom for any account of interracial sex was bound to ignite controversy. In this most conformist of times even the allegation that a young white man had taken an older Black woman as a lover went well beyond the pale. In itself, it explained the crush of onlookers who besieged the Adelaide Street courthouse and the unusually large numbers of women who daily fought to get in and revel in each forbidden detail.

Taken in the context of the times, even the suggestion that Clara Ford thought that she could marry a white man was extraordinary. Racial feelings in Canada were still influenced by the United States and in most states, North and South, it was illegal for Blacks and whites to marry. While casual liaisons between white men and Black women were accepted, if not encouraged in the South, the formal marriage of an interracial couple was a conspicuous exception.[8] As the French writer Alexis de Tocqueville noted before the Civil War, "to debauch a Negro girl hardly injures an American's reputation; to marry her dishonors him." Even after the Civil War, when a white sheriff in Mississippi married a one-eighth Black schoolteacher, the scandal was widespread and he was condemned as a "Negro-marrying" disgrace.

While Canadians might have considered themselves more enlightened, in the post-Civil War period several newspapers warned of the dangers of miscegenation and that "hybridism" would yield a backward and degenerate people. According to the Hamilton *Evening Times* of 1867, only "kindred races" should be allowed to intermarry for mixed marriages were a violation of the divine order that had created whites and Blacks as separate peoples. This continuing level of disapproval was shown by casual comments on Black-white couples in Toronto during the 1880s. These unions were, as the *World* contemptuously characterized them, "condemned by the law of God and man." Such a relationship was that of John Randolph, "a colored denizen of St. John Ward who kept a whisky dive of the lowest class which was visited by women of the most depraved type" including his companion, a white girl named Mary Murphy.[9] This fit a pattern that only an Irishwoman who had lost all sense of class or respectability would consent to become a Black man's lover. Therefore, Clara Ford's apparent assertion that she could marry any man she wanted to, even a white man, was yet another assertion of her independence and utter disregard of the norms of society.

Yet the purpose of Libby Black's testimony had been to demolish the myth of Clara Ford, the wounded heroine who had been the victim of Frank Westwood's "insult." If Black's story held up, then an alternative motive for the killing was established; that is, that Clara Ford was so insanely jealous that she threatened to shoot anyone who interfered with her love affair. Had Frank Westwood been so foolish as to attempt to break off their relationship, it was not surprising that she had resorted to violence.

Murdoch began to cross-examine her by asking about her origins as a Crown witness.[10] It all began, sordidly enough, one night after she had been arrested for public drunkenness. She approached the detectives with her story in the hopes that it would earn her some favour from the magistrate. Apparently it did and she was recommended for a light sentence. Prior to 1894 she had not known either Clara or Frank, and Frank had only identified himself to her on the occasion of their second meeting. Under further pressure by Murdoch, her testimony became evasive, and her credibility approached the vanishing point. She described Frank as wearing a dark mustache. It was apparent to everyone who had known him that Frank had been clean-shaven. Whoever Libby Black was describing in these incidents, it was certainly not Frank Westwood. Libby Black's evidence was a disaster for the prosecution, for it was patently unbelievable. As the *News* described it, "She contradicted herself half a dozen times and her attempt at the identification of either of the parties was so futile as to lead one to wonder at the nerve of the woman who would give such testimony." The attempt to ascribe the killing to feelings of jealousy had failed to the extent that it called into question the reliability of the rest of the Crown's case.

Calling Libby Black to the stand had been a serious miscalculation, and there was now a sense that the odds were shifting in Clara's favour and that even with the confession evidence she might yet escape the gallows.

CHAPTER TEN

Confessions

As the Court convened on Thursday, May 2, the Crown began its final push to prove its case. There were concerns that the sheriff and his constables could not handle the enormous crowds that besieged the tired courthouse. Every day of the trial the crowds seemed to get bigger and the *News* reported that, "Constables who serve the county of York as loyally as $1.25 per day will permit stand guard at every entrance" but despite their vigilance, "the seats are soon filled and gradually the aisles are choked up with morbid curiosity seekers."[1] As for the jurors, most of who were country folk and who would likely have preferred to be elsewhere, the strain of the trial was beginning to affect them as well. Several were complaining of illness and the poor accommodations at the Schiller Hotel. In order to give them an airing, the constables took the jury to the city gardens where, for the first time for some of them, they saw lemon and orange trees in the conservatory. It was a surprising sight to them for, "some of the county peers thought they [lemons and oranges] were sewed on. They couldn't understand how oranges and lemons could grow in Canada in May."

The difficulty for the Crown prosecution was to get these same jurors to believe that Clara Ford was a cold-blooded murderer. Still reeling from the Libby Black fiasco, the prosecutors had to endure the recall of Benjamin Westwood who swore that his son had never worn a mustache. In order to remove other suspects from contention, Osler called David Low to testify. Frank had mentioned Low in his dying moments as a friend of Gus Clark and a person who resembled the figure in the bowler hat. However, Low had a foolproof alibi for the night of the murder. Then the Crown called Gus Clark, the instigator of the accusations against Clara Ford. It turned out that this witness for the prosecution was currently serving a six-month sentence of imprisonment for stealing from his mother and was not immediately available. "Perhaps he has escaped," quipped Chancellor Boyd. The prosecution had had enough fumbling for one day and decided to go to the one witness who lay at the heart of their case. Sergeant of Detectives Henry Reburn was called to the stand.

From the moment he entered the witness stand there would be an almost continuous battle over the admissibility of his evidence. But the Sergeant, an erect, lantern-jawed figure, the veteran of twenty-two years of police service, was not about to be easily shaken. Still, the defence knew that it was crucial to keep the confession evidence from the jury and they were determined to take every step to do so. Reburn began by recounting how Clara was brought into his office about 4 o'clock on November 20. He told her that she was suspected of a serious crime and that any statement she made might be used against her. That was unnecessary, she explained, as she was completely innocent and had been elsewhere at the time of the murder. In Chancellor Boyd's trial notes he occasionally highlighted important passages and he underlined Reburn's comment, "I said that she was not bound to say anything & that anything she did say would be used in evidence against her."[2] Still the fact that he had continued to question her was proof that her initial protestation of innocence was not accepted.

Johnston instantly objected. The lawyers and the judge conferred and it was agreed that Osler would take Reburn through the circumstances leading up to the confession, the defence could cross-examine on this and the Court would then rule on its admissibility. All of this would be done with the jury present. As unusual as this may seem, no lawyer objected. Not only was it the practice for the jury to remain while procedural points were argued, all the jurors had undoubtedly read about the confession in the newspapers. Nobody entertained any illusions that this jury was a mere blank slate.

Reburn recounted how Clara had insisted she had been at the theatre. After tea, she was confronted with both Flora McKay's and Mary Crozier's stories that gave the lie to her alibi. At that point, Clara had wanted to speak, but Reburn again cautioned her. At about 10 o'clock she was moved to the commissioner's room where she insisted on making her confession to the murder. Johnston cross-examined the sergeant and wanted to know exactly when she had been arrested. Reburn could not say but when she was deposited in his office, she was not a "free agent." The entire period of interrogation and statement making had lasted till about 11:30 p.m. after which she was locked up. Throughout this cross-examination, it seemed that Johnston was laying the groundwork for the argument that his client was the victim of the "sweatbox":

> Q: She was alone there all the time, without a friend, without a lawyer?
> A: Yes.
> Q: After you got out of her what you wanted then,

the next morning you told her to see a lawyer?

A: I told her to see a lawyer.

Q: Why didn't you tell her the evening before?

A: That isn't my business.[3]

Johnston wished to leave the impression with the jury that Reburn's "business" was the extraction of confessions, not the protection of rights. Still, the sergeant insisted (and Boyd noted it), "I told her several times it would be better for her to say nothing. I said [the judge underlined the following] <u>be very careful to say nothing that is not true</u>."

If the defence could get the confession excluded, then their case was as good as won. There was so little direct evidence against Clara Ford that without the confession, a conviction was practically impossible. With the confession, the Crown did not need direct evidence, for they had the prisoner admitting to her guilt.

Johnston argued that these circumstances were different from the Day case in that Clara had not been properly arrested or advised of the charges against her before the police had started in on her. In Clara's case, the police had kept her at bay until she had confessed; anything to make them stop. Moreover, Reburn's comments, "you had better not lie" were thinly veiled threats. Chancellor Boyd would have none of it and he interrupted Johnston to state:

> I don't see why detectives should not pursue investigation by asking questions. I don't see how crimes could be followed otherwise. If the prisoner wishes to make statements I think it is proper for the detectives to question to find the truth of the statement .... Other judges think differently, I believe. English judges say that detectives should not question.[4]

Even though he knew that the tide was running against him, Johnston continued to press the point. It was a covert threat, he insisted, for Reburn to say, "If you lie to me I will have you out." The Crown was obliged to show that the statement was completely voluntary, and this was not the case. "It was revolting to one's idea of a sense of justice and fair play," Johnston insisted histrionically for poor Clara had been in police custody and plied with questions for hours, "in fact, she was on her trial."

Johnston's argument was not much different from that used by Osler only a few months previous to this in October 1894. In that case he had defended Maria Hartley on a charge of poisoning her husband. For the defence, Osler had argued, "The evidence of all constables should be taken with care. They are hunters of men and have the hunting instinct about them. They start with the conviction that a person is guilty..." On this occasion, he succeeded in discrediting the police and Maria Hartley was acquitted and left the courtroom amid an outburst of cheers. But now Osler was being retained by the prosecution. Therefore, on behalf of the police he responded that there was no indication that Reburn had threatened Clara nor offered a reward for her statement. By Canadian standards, it was admissible. Osler expressed his exasperation at Johnston's argument, "If it is a reprehensible practice for detectives to question, then the Courts should rule all confessions out, as they are not voluntary, but under the pressure of questions put by a person in authority."

Boyd had heard enough and he ruled that the confession was in. In a small concession to the defence, he decided that in the event of a conviction, they had an automatic right of appeal on the confession issue. This "stated case" to the Court of Appeal would also be a salutary lesson for, "It will be well to get an opinion of the higher court so that detectives and officers may know what to do."

The confession was in and, in a major boost to the prosecution, the jury would now hear in Clara's own words how and why she had killed Frank Westwood. Reburn continued his narrative by describing Clara's confrontations with Flora and the Croziers. When they left he took Clara to the commissioner's room and no sooner had he done so than she turned to him and said:

> Clara: There's no misleading you any longer.
> Witness: Are you going to make a statement? It will be used in evidence against you.
> Clara: I don't care. I deserve it.
> Witness: What do you mean?
> Clara: I shot Frank Westwood.
> Witness: What for?
> Clara: Because he attempted once to take improper liberties with me, and I told him that I'd get even with him.
> Witness: What about your theatre story?
> Clara: Because I did not want to give it away.[5]

She then described in precise detail how she had made her way from the Croziers' house to Dominion Street where she had hidden her dress. From there Clara had proceeded to Lakeside Hall and waited on the lawn. After seeing Frank go in she waited another 15 or 20 minutes and then went up and rang the doorbell. When Frank answered, she fired the shot. It was never her intention to kill, she insisted, only to wound. Then she related how she had retraced her steps to Dominion Street and from there along the lakefront and across the New Fort grounds to downtown. Occasionally she interjected that she had never intended to kill but that, "Frank Westwood and the other boys had teased her and persecuted her because of her colour and because she sometimes wore men's clothes" and she felt that some response was warranted.

As Sergeant Reburn described her motive as she told it to him, it

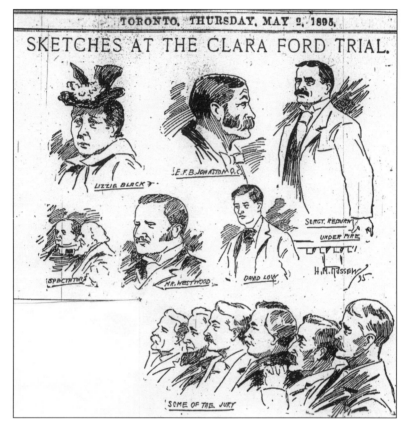

Trial scene as sketched for the Toronto News, *May 2, 1895.*

seemed to have far more to do with teasing and taunts than with any attempted rape. Clara's story that Frank had "insulted" her might be literally that, that she had been offended by rude remarks and slights rather than with any sexual assault. Blackie Johnston did his best to shake Reburn's account, but it was a telling point that he could accomplish little. In hours of cross-examination the policeman stuck to his story and there were few inconsistencies to be winkled out. Johnston got Reburn to agree that he had said that Clara had passed through the gates of Exhibition Park. Thinking he had scored a point, Johnston advised the sergeant that the gates were closed at that time of night. Not so, corrected Reburn. He had talked with the Exhibition staff who told him that they did not bother to close these particular gates. Johnston read out a portion of the record taken during the Police Court proceedings before Colonel Denison where Reburn had stated that Clara had passed along the New Fort and along the waterfront. This report was wrong, Reburn corrected him, and she had gone through the Old Fort, not along the lakefront. Still, it was an inconsistency and Johnston avidly worked the point:

> Q: Did she go in front of the New Fort or back of it?
> A: Across the waterfront.
> Q: Did she ever tell you that she passed in front of the New Fort?

Mr. Johnston then read the evidence of the sergeant at the Police Court in which he swore she said she passed in front of the New Fort. "It's not right," said the witness. "It's taken down wrong." "Then its false," said Mr. Johnston. "That's the third occasion in which you differ from the evidence reported here."[6]

> Q: Didn't you tell Clara Ford that night that she was on trial for her life?
> A: I don't remember it if I did.
> Q: Will you swear you didn't?
> A: No.
> Q: Are you afraid of being contradicted by this? (Holding up Police Court evidence)
> A: No, I am not afraid of anything.
> Q: Not even in the face of the contradictions you have already made?
> A: No![7]

Bitter exchanges such as this broke out regularly during the cross-examination. "Why," Johnston asked, "had the sergeant never made enquiries at the Opera House to see if her original story was true?" "What was the point," he shot back, "she had already confessed to murder." This was the crucial moment, and Johnston could only hope that at least to some extent Reburn's credibility had been diminished in the eyes of the jury. How would they like to have endured hours of questioning at the hands of this determined detective?

Inspector William Stark was next on the stand, and he recounted how after the confession had been made to Reburn he had taken Clara into his office where he had also cautioned her that, "there was a serious charge against her and that she had better not say anything." Resigned to her fate, she replied, "there is no use in my denying it any longer" and she had described the incident exactly as she had related it to the sergeant. When Stark asked her why she had shot the young man, she responded that she liked to spend her spare time in Parkdale but, "her colour prevented her from going about much, and she used to go to that locality to sit and read." Frank Westwood and his chums had harassed her and on one occasion "he met her there, and caught hold of her about the waist and threw her down, attempting to assault her." As for the route, Stark swore that he had gone over it twice and part of it three times. It was entirely feasible to walk this line. The inspector was also subjected to an intensely probing cross-examination. The thrust of Blackie Johnston's questions was to imply that the police tactics had coerced the confession:

> Q: Did she tell you that she had a struggle in the hallway of the Westwood's house?
> A: No.
> Q: Did you question her so as to make the evidence of the Crown complete?

A: No, I wanted to get at the facts, so as to clear up the mystery.[8]

Johnston asked for the police book to be produced. After it was handed to him, he showed it to Stark and asked him to note that Clara had been officially arrested at 11:40 p.m. on the night of November 20:

> Q: Why was this woman kept in the detective department from 4 o'clock to 11:40?
> A: To make enquiries for the purpose of finding out whether we had sufficient evidence to make a charge of murder.[9]

"To make enquiries of her?" Johnston asked histrionically. The point was not to illicit information, but to underline to the jury that she had been under intense police questioning for almost eight hours. During this grilling, a *Telegram* reporter thought that, "The court room became insufferably close. The barristers mopped their faces with their handkerchiefs and the crowd sweltered... a very sharp passage ensued between the Q.C. and the inspector." Yet, throughout this, the irritated inspector kept his temper and had again demonstrated the consistency and clarity of the confession evidence.

Whatever its merits, Clara Ford's confession was now a matter of record. As the *Globe* described it, even after Johnston's blistering cross-examinations, "the main facts of the story remained unshaken, and left the confession in all its damning completeness against the prisoner."[10]

CHAPTER ELEVEN

Ribbons and Bullets

The remainder of the Crown's case was anticlimatic. The elusive Gus Clark had been found. However, he could add little to the case beyond observing that he had often seen Frank Westwood at the boathouse on Lake Ontario and that for a time Clara Ford had lived nearby. The only purpose behind his being called seemed to be to eliminate him as one of the suspects. The defence accepted this and only cross-examined him on his relationship with Clara. "I knew the prisoner" he admitted, "I found her a good, decent girl."[1] Yet, Clark's evidence was so tangential to the issues that most wondered why the authorities had bothered to remove him from the quiet of his prison cell.

The same could not be said of the next witness, Christian Dorenwend, an individual previously unconnected to the affair.[2] Dorenwend was the husband of one of the Clark girls and his evidence came in the form of two letters whose curious contents seemed to bind the prisoner to her victim. As B.B. Osler prepared to open the letters, Dorenwend hastily appealed to the Court to keep them secret for the contents would seriously prejudice the reputation of several fine ladies. Chancellor Boyd appreciated the gravity of this and ordered Osler to omit any public reference to the ladies. For his part Johnston felt that as these letters were written four years previously they could not possibly have any relevance. But the trial judge, like most observers, had his curiosity piqued by these documents and he insisted that Osler produce them.

Both letters referred back to the confrontation on the Clark verandah in May 1890. On that occasion, Clara Ford had made strong accusations against the Clark girls and for this she had been banished from the household. Now Dorenwend picked up two letters signed by a "Jim Hardy," but which the Crown suggested was in Clara's handwriting. The contents of the letters were so scandalous that none of Toronto's dailies would print the contents in full. No such sensibilities troubled Chancellor Boyd and in his personal trial notes he recorded some of the contents. The first letter of May 14 stated, "G. is a regular whore. She used lust… by talking before all the boys: ask Westwood's Frank. She is crazy after him – there is no young lady in the village will be seen with her."[3] And two days later the same person wrote, "Young Westwood told me that this week – were asking their hired man to take them to the theatre." Dorenwend had acted as deputy to the Clark family in confronting Clara Ford with these letters and accusing her of being the author. Not surprisingly, she had stood her ground, admitted that she had written them and that every word was true. Upon learning of Clara's arrest, Dorenwend had turned the letters over to the police.

The significance of the letters lay, not in showing any bad feelings between Clara and Frank, but rather that they had known each other well enough that Frank was twice cited as the source of her information. It showed a strange intimacy between the two: between

14-year-old Frank from a good family and 28-year-old Clara, an uneducated Black woman who until recently had been travelling alone about the Midwest. These letters showed that this unlikely couple had formed a peculiar companionship in which Clara could confidently cite young Frank as a source to back up her accusations.

As the prosecution neared its conclusion it came upon yet another misfortune. During the evening of May 3, Carrie Osler, who had never fully recovered from her injuries sustained during the gas fire of 1874, died at home. The following morning, the assistant Crown attorney, Hartley Dewart, advised the Court that B.B. Osler could not continue. It was Osler who was most familiar with all the details of the case, particularly the still anticipated evidence on the condition of the bullet, and without him the prosecution would be handicapped. As the Hamilton *Spectator* phrased it, Osler's withdrawal was "a severe shock to the authorities. Mr. Osler's able counsel work was doing a great deal towards weaving the web of circumstantial evidence about the prisoner."[4] In light of this, Dewart pleaded for an adjournment. Dewart was a capable young man, but had only been called to the bar for eight years and he carried none of Osler's *gravitas* before a jury. It probably did not come as a surprise to him when Boyd ruled that as the case was so far advanced that it could not be stopped or a new jury empanelled. The prosecution, would have to present the all-important ballistics evidence with lawyers who were only sketchily familiar with its details.

The remaining Crown lawyers, Dewart and Curry, seemed unsure of just where the case was headed. The next four witnesses, all Jewish and all part of the millinery trade, contributed little to the cause and to some extent detracted from it. Clara's employer, Samuel Barnett, added nothing to the Crown's case but to Murdoch he confirmed that:

> A: "Her conduct couldn't be beat: she didn't want
> to be bothered by anyone when she was at work.

Benjamin Vise taking his oath,
Toronto News, *May 3, 1895.*

Q: Has she a temper?
A: She got a high temper. There's no use talkin'; we
all got high tempers ain't we?5

Before coming to Barnett's, Clara had worked for Benjamin
Vise, the same talkative tailor who had given such a vivid interview
to the *World* reporters. He now repeated the story of how one day he
had accidentally knocked down her coat. It landed with such a
thump that he was surprised and investigated to find that there was
a revolver in one of the pockets. In one of the trial's lighter
moments, Vise recounted his horror at even having to touch the
pistol. Amid laughter from the crowd, Vise said that, "I never handled a revolver in my life and I didn't want a girl who carried a
revolver." Vise asked Clara what she was doing with the weapon and
she responded that it was for her protection. She then told him:

"I suppose you will see me married some day."

"To whom?" Vise asked.

"Gus Clarke."

"Gus Clarke," cried Vise in surprise. "Will Gus marry a colored girl?"[6]

It was a natural enough question. Any white man who contemplated an interracial marriage in the 1890s had better be prepared for a social reaction. She answered:

> "He [Gus Clark] took me buggy riding every night. If he doesn't, I'll do him up as I did a man in the States."

Taken aback, a frightened Vise told her to look for work elsewhere. Reaction to this evidence was also instructive, for the *Telegram* noted, "Some of this evidence seemed to amuse the prisoner very much, especially that part about marrying Gus Clark. She laughed considerably about it." The implication was that Clara did not consider Gus Clark worthy of her.

At this point, the spectators were treated to a gorgeous display of the millinery arts as two of Clara's colleagues in the ribbon trade were called to the stand. Jennie Bloom wore a bonnet composed of purple ribbons and convolvulus. If women's fashion in the 1890s still required the confining laced-up corset, there was nothing preventing women from adorning the exterior with ribbon and colour. Jennie had worked in a tailor shop with Clara and on occasion had seen her with a revolver. Clara explained that a man had tried to assault her and that as she had to pass by the same route she carried it for protection. Gussie Cohen, who sported a hat trimmed with terra cotta ribbons and surmounted by jets of feathers that nodded to both judge and jurors as she testified, confirmed that Clara did more than just carry the revolver. On one occasion at the shop her temper had gotten the best of her and she had warned, "If anybody did her any harm she would do him up."

Finally the Crown presented that piece of evidence that, next to the confession, it hoped would secure a conviction. William Elliott, a lifelong gun-maker, took the stand.[7] He had examined the revolver taken from Clara's room and explained that it had a defect in the barrel, a "burr" near the muzzle. Moreover, the connection between the barrel and the firing chamber was not true and the bullet would strike a projection when fired. Lastly, the .38 calibre bullets were too small for the barrel and would oscillate as they left the chamber and exit the weapon at an angle with little penetrating power. He then produced the fatal ball and explained that the marks on the side of the bullet matched those from a bullet fired from Clara Ford's weapon. The bullet was then handed around to the jury members along with a magnifying glass to enable them to see the marks for themselves. In a stage door aside that could likely be heard by all the jurors, Johnston quipped, "The Crown's evidence was so minute that it required a magnifying glass to discover."[8]

Despite Johnston's irony, this should have been persuasive evidence. The relatively soft metal of the bullet was susceptible to being marked by the tiniest variations in the machined surface of the barrel or of the breech-face. As these surfaces were never completely smooth, they would inevitably leave a distinctive pattern, a profile of the inner surface of the gun barrel, on the bullet itself. In modern ballistics tests, a round is fired into an extended box of cotton wadding or a container of water in which to catch the bullet in an undamaged condition. Then, the test bullet can be compared to the suspect one through a powerful microscope in a divided field comparison. So long as the suspect projectile is in good condition a definitive comparison can be made and a weapon either confirmed or cleared as the one responsible.[9] This level of sophistication was not available to Toronto police in 1895. Elliott described the tests he had

One of Clara's defenders,
W.G. Murdoch, Toronto Empire,
Nov. 29, 1894.

made; firing Clara's revolver into a side of beef covered with two shirts and a vest. One bullet was fired from distances of eight and twenty feet and in each instance the bullets struck sideways and flattened out in the flesh. These test shots resulted in bullets on which "the marks were identical as those in the Westwood bullet." Instead of a microscope, Elliott used a regular magnifying glass to make the comparisons. Chancellor Boyd recorded in his notes that the test bullets showed "the same little scratches as on the Westwood bullet."[10] Elliott then repeated the test using a revolver of similar make. For starters, there was much more direct force to the shot and the round passed straight through the meat. Moreover, the marks on these other projectiles were not at all similar to those on the Westwood bullet.

The jurors examined all of these test bullets with interest. As several of them were country people and likely used firearms on a regular basis, this aspect of the case piqued their interest. If arcane legal arguments on the admissibility of statements left them cold, this was an issue they likely felt they could judge for themselves. On the face of it, the definitive nature of Elliott's investigation linking the murder to the weapon found in Clara's room seemed to have plugged any gaps and put the Crown's case over the top. Whatever misfortunes it had encountered along the way, a foolproof case now seemed to have been made.

Yet before the Crown lawyers could sit back and savour their triumph, William Elliott would be subject to cross-examination. To Murdoch he confirmed that the revolver, a "British Bulldog," was of a cheap make and that he had seen about 50,000 such weapons. Made of malleable cast iron, each one in this series would have had the same burr on the barrel, as did Clara's pistol. There were thousands of such revolvers in Toronto. Chancellor Boyd highlighted Elliott's next comment in his notes, "I have seen plenty of such revolvers as this with the same defect."[11] A fellow gunsmith, George Oakley, tried to back up Elliott's opinion but only seemed to add to the uncertainty. Oakley could not even confirm the exact calibre of the bullet nor could he tell if it was eighteen months or three months since the weapon had been fired. The only thing he could say with any certainty was that one chamber had been fired more recently than the others. At this point one of the jurors interjected and asked if they might see some tests done on these weapons. The judge agreed and that evening the jury observed the experts test firing the revolvers. The end result of this expert testimony, as the *World* observed, was, "not that the Westwood bullet must necessarily have been fired from the prisoner's revolver, but that the prisoner possessed a weapon which could have fired a similar bullet."[12] After all this effort, painfully little had been proven.

For good or ill, this was the full extent of the Crown's case and Hartley Dewart rose to announce, "That's the case for the Crown, my Lord."

With the Crown's case all in, Johnston rose for one last try to throw out the confession. After what they had now heard, he argued that the "confession" was the product of such duress and police mis-conduct that it should be excluded. Predictably, Boyd ruled that it would stay. Yet this was not an entirely futile gesture, for it enabled Johnston to state (in front of the jury) the theme that he would repeat throughout the defence case; that is that the real question was how the police treated the suspects in their custody. It was this issue that would become the bedrock of the defence case and, if properly developed, would show Clara as the victim not the perpetrator of an injustice.

CHAPTER TWELVE

Clara's Version

That Thursday afternoon, May 3, W.G. Murdoch began the case for the defence. An excited ripple went through the spectators when he rose and simply announced, "I call the prisoner, my Lord."[1]

Coughs and shuffles in the densely packed courtroom ceased as Clara Ford walked without hesitation into the witness stand, took the oath and with a flourish kissed the Bible. As she began her testimony (only the second accused murderer in Toronto to have that chance), she was deliberately and defiantly provocative. Denied access to a better world, she had developed a barbed repartee as a form of protection and throughout her testimony she would exhibit a ferocious vigour that captivated the crowd.

She began by relating how she had been born in Toronto 33 years before and how her parents had died when she was a child. This seemed to be in contrast with every other account of her origins as a foundling. Nevertheless, there was no disputing her account of earning her own way in the world since the age of 12 or 13. The previous November she had been at her work at Barnett's when two men came in and began to whisper to her employer. Then one of them, whom she now knew to be Detective Slemin, came over to her and asked to see her room. She asked why, and he said, "in a coaxing sort of way that he just wanted to see the room." She suspected that they were detectives but did not know what they were after. Detective Porter asked if she had men's clothing and whether she had worn them in Parkdale disguised as an old man. Clara denied that she had ever gone out in such a disguise. Slemin followed this up by asking if she had a revolver. "This has something to do with the Westwood tragedy," she blurted out. It was just the first thing that came to her mind. The policemen retrieved the revolver from the bottom of her trunk where she said it had lain since before August. She explained that she had bought the pistol and six bullets from "a second-hand Jew on York Street for $1.50" and that "in a spirit of devilment" she had once fired two bullets at some ducks.

That was enough for the detectives. "Inspector Stark wants to see you downtown," announced Slemin. They bundled up the clothes, and Slemin dropped her revolver in his pocket. Leaving the drudgery of the tailor shop behind, Clara and the two officers walked to the central police station where Clara was deposited in the office of Sergeant Henry Reburn.

She vividly described their first encounter and the spectators strained to hear every word. "He came in and gave me a look as if he would snatch my head off; oh, he didn't talk as he did yesterday. He said 'Where did you get those pants? Where were you that Saturday night?' He had a rougher and snappier voice than he had here yesterday." The sergeant then stated that she was seen in Parkdale that night. She denied it. She had not been in Parkdale since last Civic Holiday in August 1894. Did she know Frank Westwood? This she denied as well. At no time during this rapid fire exchange of questions and answers had Reburn ever told her that her words could be used against her.

At one point, Inspector Stark came in and began to question her on her background. She had been born in Toronto, she insisted, and was "half-Spanish." "What were you doing with men's clothes?" the inspector queried. "That is against the law." A defiant Clara responded, "If that is so, how is it that Vic Steinberg [the popular features writer for the Toronto *News*]² goes to baseball matches and down to the opera and wears men's clothes and nothing is said about it?" As she described it, "The inspector stroked his moustache and smiled a little, but didn't answer."

After Reburn and Stark had a short conference, Stark left and let the sergeant go back to work. He fired a barrage of questions at her concerning her activities on the night of October 6. It was simple, she explained. At 7:15 that night she had met Flora McKay at the corner of Bay and Queen and together they had walked to the Opera House. Clara bought the 35-cent tickets and they took their seats in the balcony. After the show they walked up Yonge Street where Clara had noticed on the Wanless clock that it was about 10:30. They walked past the Simpson's store where she bought a Sunday *World* and proceeded to Richmond Street where Flora lived. Before they parted, Clara instructed Flora to tell her landlady that they had been at the theatre together and that was the reason she was home late. Clara arrived back at her room at Mrs. Dorsay's at 10:45 that evening.

It was an incredibly detailed recollection, especially considering the amount of time that had elapsed. Clara recalled which part of the balcony they had sat in and that Flora had been wearing a light dress, cape and a tam-o'-shanter cap. The sergeant was not impressed:

"You're making all this up." he said

"No, I ain't; it's the truth," she insisted.

"Well" he responded, "You needn't get saucy about it."

The thoroughly aroused Clara retorted, "Well, I've got a right to speak up when I'm telling you the truth."

It was getting dark and Reburn escorted her to the matron's room where she took some refreshment. He left and locked the door behind him.

After about an hour he returned and the questioning resumed in earnest. When was the last time she had worn men's clothing? "Over a year ago," she replied. When she had visited the Crozier's? What had she done with the black fedora? She had given it away to one of the Crozier boys the previous September. She insisted that she had never owned a fake moustache. During the questioning, Reburn would occasionally leave to consult with other detectives who were on the street gathering additional information. Finally, in order to get her position clear, Reburn asked "Are you sure you were at the Opera House?" She answered, "Yes I was." The sergeant then played one of his trump cards "The little girl said that you told her to say that you were at the Opera House."

"My God, she is telling a lie," was Clara's response.

Reburn then had her repeat her earlier assertion that she did not know Frank. To undermine this part of her story, the detective pulled out the recently acquired "Jim Hardy" letters in which the author (presumably Clara) had listed "Westwood's Frank" as the source of her information. Equivocally, and not very convincingly, she told him that she could not swear that she did not write the letters, but she knew where they came from. Reburn was making considerable headway in undermining her alibi and now it was Slemin's turn. He entered the room and began to fire questions at her about the Crozier family:

> You were not at the Opera, Clara. Mrs. Crozier says that you were at her house that night and you were drunk and your coat was open and you had a revolver.

> She is lying, Clara said, send for her to come and I'll
> show you I was at the Opera.

There was no need for that as the police already had the Crozier family secured in an adjacent room. It was one of the high points of her testimony when Clara described the scene as Mary Crozier and her daughter Sadie were brought into the interrogation room. Clara described how the women:

> Looked around as if they were half-scared to death...
> Clara laughed immoderately as the scene recurred
> to her and rolled her eyes and struck attitudes illus-
> trative of those alleged to have been assumed by the
> Croziers. She repeatedly grinned during this recital.[3]

Mrs. Crozier began to talk about Clara being at their place on Camden Street till about 9 o'clock. "It's a lie," Clara interjected. Reburn put up his hand and said "Shut up, now." Mary Crozier completed her recollection and Clara was taken to yet another room. But it was the manner in which Clara described the interchange that captivated the courtroom. For once in her life this obscure seamstress held the undivided attention of hundreds of people. Her words would be quoted by all the city's dailies the following morning. Instead of buying balcony seats to a melodrama she was the headliner in a critical performance. Vivid expression was never a problem for Clara Ford. Not only was she the star of the drama, she colourfully acted out the other parts from the terrified Croziers to the intimidating detectives. Occasionally, and inappropriately, she burst out in laughter as she described the reaction of the other participants.

How did the courtroom audience react to the performance? As the *World* (a newspaper which was unremittingly hostile to her)

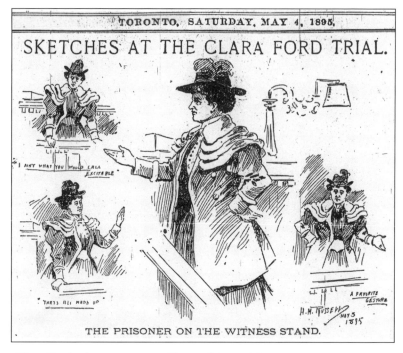

Clara Ford takes centre stage, Toronto News, *May 4, 1895.*

described it, she gave her testimony in a flippant manner. "Standing in a masculine attitude, with her arms akimbo after the manner of her race, she glibly rattled off her story, with a minuteness of detail which showed that observation can supplement, stimulate and strengthen imagination to an incredible degree."[4] The jurors must have read the newspaper accounts of her from the previous fall about her strange origins and stranger lifestyle. From these reports they would have heard all the accounts of this bizarre and aggressive man/woman. The jury was a collection of respectable wagon-makers, painters, weavers and blacksmiths who came, for the most part, from outside the city. It is likely that most of them rarely if ever saw a Black person. Their experience of Blacks came, if at all, from the crude caricatures in minstrel shows where Blacks were portrayed as slow, childish figures unable to understand the consequences of their actions. In her testimony, Clara Ford seemed to be meeting these low expectations for she displayed an almost instinctive understanding of the nuances of race and class. Where she should have been serious, she was glib. Where she should have been respectful of authority (one of the policemen who was in civilian clothes she referred to as "white pants") she was teasing. Was she acting (consciously or unconsciously) in the anticipated "manner of her race" to conform to the jury's expectations of how she should act – that is childish, stupid and ultimately unable to take responsibility for what she did, even if it was murder?

Whatever her motive, her performance was reaching its climax as she recounted how she was relocated yet again to the commissioner's office. Reburn shut the windows, drew down the blinds and closed the inside green baize doors. Now she was truly cut off from the outer world. Almost as soon as she got there Reburn drew up a chair, sidled up beside her and struck a friendlier tone. "Clara if you don't tell the truth it will be worse for you."[5] Then he paced about the room and again sat down next to her. "If you were my own sister I couldn't think more of you." She replied that she had nothing to say. "Only say that he insulted you," Reburn offered. "He's dead now and can't say anything. There's $500 or $600 offered for the case," he said with a wink. Ominously, he added "If you don't tell the truth it would be worse for you."

The crowd, which had, for the most part been quiet, or occasionally chuckling along with Clara's impersonations, suddenly gasped. Her version was that the police had concocted the entire confession. Frank Westwood had never "insulted" her nor had she killed Frank. The entire confession was a police sham to solve the mystery and register a conviction.

As she described it, Reburn continued his seductive chat, "Clara, its getting late; I can't bother with you no more tonight; if you were a man I'd not bother with you; I'd put you downstairs; Clara, you got yourself in a net and you can't get out of it." She had reached her limits.

"At last he kept worrying me so I said I did do it. And then I made up this lie."

"You mean the alleged confession," prompted Murdoch.

"Yes" she replied. "I made up this lie to get out of trouble. I made up the shooting from a picture I saw in the papers and from what Mrs. Crozier said. It is a false story."

So now, after Murdoch and Johnston had done everything possible to exclude the confession, the defence was now conceding that this was exactly the story she had given to the police. Only now she took the stance that it was all an invention, a product of police intimidation and chicanery. She described how Stark had come into the interrogation chamber and suggested details to her, "You met Frank at a fence, you were struggling at the fence and you got this revolver and shot him." She agreed with this and the inspector added cryptically, "There cannot be anything done to you." Reburn added "Now, you stick to it, don't change your mind. Stick to one story." Before she was arrested and locked up, she asked Reburn if he intended to broadcast this story. "Not to a living soul," he assured her.

"And what did he mean by telling me that lie?" she asked while, in the *Globe's* description, "gesticulating wildly."

Perhaps fearing that she was overplaying her hand, Murdoch nudged her, "Never mind that, go on."

Clara denied that she had ever been at the Crozier's at all but that she had dropped by on the Monday night after the tragedy. Yes, she had carried a revolver, but never a loaded one. Libby Black's testimony was a lie and she had never even talked to Frank Westwood. It was slightly more than two hours since she had come to the stand. It was a bravura performance. But was it enough?

In cross-examination by Dewart, Clara stuck stubbornly to this, her most recent version, and along the way took a few energetic sideswipes at the detectives. She insisted that they had never cautioned her. Inspector Stark had not taken down her confession, rather he had done all the talking and she had simply agreed. The police statements were true in all their detail. She had simply made it all up as Reburn was "worrying her" and she desperately wanted to escape his grasp. However, she did admit to sending the obscene letters to the Clarks. Was this not an admission that she had known Frank Westwood? Other than this, she stuck to the story she had given in chief.[6] Dewart asked her what could have caused her putative daughter Flora to lie against her mother. On this rare occasion Clara had no answer. She simply shrugged and said, "I can't account for Flora saying she was not with me on Saturday at the Opera." The entire Crozier family, Flora McKay and all of the police officers had been lying. Every witness so far, even those who were her closest friends, had perjured themselves. Only she spoke the truth; and that truth she stubbornly maintained was that she had spent that Saturday evening watching *The Black Crook* with Flora. She had not known Frank Westwood and had nothing to do with his murder.

A few interesting details did emerge from the cross-examination. She was a married woman. About ten years previously, she had married a man in Chicago, lived with him for a year but had not seen him since.

Calling Clara as the first witness had been a bold tactical gamble for the defence. Had the confession been excluded, there was practically no direct evidence against her and the defence would never have taken the risk of putting her on the stand. But in the circumstances they had to adopt an aggressive posture to refute the confession. The question was, should they persist in the line first advanced by Clara that she had been protecting her honour? Carolyn Strange has suggested that Johnston would be treading on, "shaky ground if he tried to convince the jury that his client had shot a respectable white man because he had tried to rape her."[7] Therefore, the defence lawyers shifted ground and took an inventive approach, that, "she had made an easy target for unchivalrous detectives who had badgered her and duped her into making a false confession." The prosecution would get no advance notice of this new strategy and would be hard-pressed to come up with fresh evidence (such as witnesses who could prove that Clara and Frank knew each other) to counteract it. This analysis also pre-supposes that Johnston invented an entirely new defence story and fed it, word by word, into his client's mouth.

At 5:30 that evening she stepped down from the stand as the *Globe* described it, "with the same jaunty, devil-may-care air which had characterized her entry into the box."[8] The *World* assured its readers that her account was rife with contradictions. The jury was being asked to believe that she had deliberately given the police a detailed (but false) story of how she had killed Frank Westwood simply to stop their questioning. This latest fiction was the product of a few observations, "on which her imagination acted. It furnished the spark that kindled the imagination into flame and the flame grandly blowed and burned for over three hours." To the *World*, Clara's testimony was mere theatrics for they felt that:

> The laughing way in which she alluded to the frightened condition of the witnesses who were brought to confront her showed that she relished the notoriety she was receiving. She had admired and envied weekly the heroines in the plays at the theaters, and she enjoyed the fact that she was at length the central figure in a drama.[9]

To the *Telegram*, however, these were not theatrics but the sincere recollection of a falsely accused woman. At this late stage in the drama, the truth was finally being presented to the Court. According to the *Telegram*, Clara had given a compelling performance.[10] The crowd had hung on her every word, which words had "created a most favourable impression on her behalf judging from the comments made in the crowd" and which had been offered with "an emphasis that carried conviction with it and she gave every little particular about the case that added to the strength of her statements."

When the Court resumed on Saturday morning it was apparent that the pace of the trial was quickening and that the conclusion was near.

CHAPTER THIRTEEN

Final Battle

At times, it seemed as if the struggle for Clara Ford's life had evolved into a subscription battle between the newspapers. On the one hand, Toronto readers were enthralled by the *World* and its colourful descriptions of Clara as a crazed murderess. The *World's* counterpart in the penny daily market, the *Telegram* (described by one of its competitors as "the autocrat of Toronto newspapers") reported each day of the trial in exceptional detail and laid as much emphasis as it could on evidence that favoured Clara. The slightly more expensive *Globe* struck a higher tone and reported the evidence with no apparent interest in the outcome. An editorial in the *News* warned that "trial by newspaper" was becoming all too common.[1] Journalists were getting news tips from detectives who then expected the newspapers to support their actions. The *News* felt that this was an unhealthy situation that could result in accused persons (perhaps even Clara Ford) being "publicly branded as murderers before their trial commences." The newspapers were about to go beyond any pretense of objectivity and, in one of the trial's more bizarre moments, become active participants in the drama.

It began that Saturday morning while the jurors were test firing Clara's revolver. Johnston drew Chancellor Boyd's attention to the previous day's article in the *World*. It was so malicious and unfair that he asked the judge to take criminal action against the newspaper.[2] While seeming to agree with Blackie Johnston that the article was scurrilous, Boyd decided to leave the prosecution (if any) in the hands of the attorney general. In any case, Boyd reminded Johnston that the jury was not permitted to read the papers and even if the report was unfair that it could not impact on the trial's outcome.

If the *World* was the villain of the piece, according to the defence, the *Telegram* was without blemish. George Bennett, the city editor of that newspaper, was called to the stand and he recounted how he had his reporters trace Clara Ford's route. Two staffers, a reporter, Charles Clark, and an artist and engraver, W.J. Thompson, walked the path and reported back that the water was so high in front of the New Fort that it was next to impossible that Clara could have traversed it. The water, which lapped up to the fort's bastions, masked a field of boulders. Not only was this difficult to cross, the bastion itself was a twelve-foot-high wall topped by barbed wire. The reporters concluded that, "at night as was suggested by the detective; it would be difficult to go around: it would be almost impossible to wade around in the water as the shore goes down steeply."[3] Bennett recounted how after the *Telegram* had delivered this pronouncement that put the police account into question, he received a surprise visit from none other than Sergeant Reburn. The sergeant doggedly argued the point with Bennett and he asked why the police were being doubted when their conclusions were so compelling. "He [Reburn] seemed to be very candid," Bennett recalled, "and gave witness the impression that he believed in the feasibility of the route."

Chloe Dorsay, landlady,
Toronto News, May 4, 1895.

Nevertheless, George Bennett stuck by the information as given to him by his staff.

One of the following witnesses, Clara's landlady Chloe Dorsay, was only the second Black person to make an appearance in the case.[4] Despite her advanced age, she rivalled Clara in feistiness and determination. A stout, matronly woman with a round, jovial face, Mrs. Dorsay wore a black dress highlighted by two violets in her cap. She distinctly recalled the night of October 6 when Clara, wearing a new jacket, had left between seven and eight that night. She had returned to 152 York Street "about eleven or a little after." Through her spectacles, Mrs. Dorsay had seen the girl arrive home and recalled Clara saying good night before going upstairs. As for the detectives, they had invaded her little boarding house/restaurant and appeared "awful imperint." She described with glee how Slemin and Porter had discovered a black bottle they suspected of being illegal liquor. Laughingly, she recounted the look on their faces when they discovered that it was only coal oil. "At the recital of this joke on the officers, the old lady looked up and gurgled at His Lordship in the most engaging way." When she admitted that she was unsure of her own birthplace, "the Chancellor smiled for the first time since the trial opened." Much like Clara Ford's conduct in the witness box, Chloe Dorsay's testimony seemed tailored to meet what a respectable white audience would expect from a Black witness.

Yet it also seemed designed to add a few more brush strokes to the picture of police misconduct that the defence was painting. When the police had first burst in and questioned Clara, Mrs. Dorsay's daughter Mamie had tried to speak up. One of the detectives shouted at her, "Shut up, or I'll take you in the patrol." These were the same Toronto police who vigorously enforced the liquor laws and who arrested little boys who played baseball on Sundays. How believable was Mrs. Dorsay's story and how much sympathy was it generating for the defence?

Perhaps even more than Clara, Mrs. Dorsay was an original on the witness stand. Hartley Dewart attempted to cross-examine her on one point and asked:

> Q: Is Clara hot-tempered?
> A: Not any more than you.
> Q: Did you ever see me hot?
> A: You're getting hot now.[5]

"Listen, Mrs. Crozier" said the momentarily flustered Dewart. "Mrs. Crozier!" shouted the landlady "Don't call me that name."

Not only had she won that exchange, she also prevailed over Chancellor Boyd. He had noted her comment that she had seen Clara arrive home "through her spectacles."[6] Could she actually read? The judge doubted it and it is perhaps not surprising that in his stereotypical view, Black persons such as Mrs. Dorsay were dismissed as illiterate. Boyd asked her to read a label off a bottle.

Although she was clearly incensed at the imputation that she could not read, she did so:

"Very well done," said the Chancellor.

"Why, did you think I couldn't read?" demanded Mrs. Dorsay as she flounced out of the courtroom. For those who were paying close attention to the evidence, the stereotypes of Black residents of the Ward should have been diminishing. Not only was Mrs. Dorsay literate, Clara had mentioned several times that she was an avid newspaper and book reader who read several of the dailies. As many Crown witnesses had observed she was also an excellent worker, neither lazy nor stupid. The popular minstrel-show depiction of Blacks was not consistent with the actual Black residents who appeared before the Court.

Still, there was no doubt that while Mrs. Dorsay would do everything in her power to help Clara, she was frequently confused. She insisted on calling the victim "Clark" and resented being corrected on the point. She could not recall if she had been in Court two days previously. One other detail in her testimony almost escaped notice yet said volumes about the defence. She agreed with Clara that it was Monday that she had brought her laundry home from Mrs. Crozier's, but added a fatal detail:

> Clara told her that she had gone to the Crozier's house that Saturday, October 6 and that Mrs. Crozier had tried to borrow money from her.

This corroborated Mary Crozier's testimony that Clara had been at their house on Saturday and refuted Clara's story that she had never been there at all on Saturday. A defence witness had, unwittingly, given strong credence to the Crown's case. However, it was only a passing detail and was never to be exploited by the prosecution.

The other Black residents of Mrs. Dorsay's establishment did what they could to bolster Clara's alibi. Eliza Reid, a waitress and fellow boarder, recalled that Clara had on a new jacket that evening and announced that she was going to wear it to the show. Eliza also remembered Clara coming home sometime around eleven o'clock. Mrs. Dorsay's daughter Mamie also said that Clara had stepped out that evening but did not see her return. At that point, a squad of employees from the Toronto Opera House was called to try to secure the alibi. William Meldum, an usher, swore that he had seen Clara at the October 6 performance. Closer questioning revealed that he believed this as she usually came to the Saturday show and that "the impression I have is that it was Saturday night." The Opera House's detective, James McLaughlin, was even more vague. He thought that he saw Clara at the performance of *The Black Crook*, but could not recall on which day. In any event, he was sure that she was alone. William Graham, a ticket seller, recognized Clara as a frequent the-atre-goer. He recalled seeing her in the balcony and these seats were only sold on Saturday nights. Equivocal evidence such as this was a fragile reed upon which to base an alibi. This was so even when the persons who put forth these stories were so emphatic. Eliza Reid, for one, swore that Clara was back at York Street at the time of the murder. "There is no doubt about it," she assured the jury.

The prosecution did doubt it and, in reply, the detectives were recalled to the stand. Inspector Stark, perhaps the city's most impos-ing officer next to Chief Constable Grasett himself, swore that Clara Ford's account of what transpired on the night of November 20 was a complete lie. At no point had he ever counselled her to invent a story or written down a false story for her to attest to. Sergeant Reburn also denied that there was any inducements made to her and denied that she had been coerced in any way. As for Mrs. Dorsay's testimony, Slemin had talked with her just after Clara had been arrested and at that time the old lady said that she had no idea when Clara had arrived home. She added that on Saturday nights the hall door was usually open until 12:30 or thereabouts. Clara could easily have entered the boarding house at that time and gone up to her room undetected. Porter corroborated this and added that Mrs. Dorsay's conviction that Clara had come back by around 11:00 was a story of rather fresh vintage. Chancellor Boyd noted, "Mrs. Dorsay said she did not know when Clara Ford came in on the night of 6 October."[6]

This completed the evidence. To contemporary eyes, the speed of the trial was nothing less than extraordinary. A century later, a murder trial could easily take a month or more and feature lengthy arguments on Charter of Rights issues. However, in the 1890s, there were many instances of murder trials being conducted from start to sentence of death in a day. Clara Ford's trial consumed five days and was, by the standards of the day, a long one. The large number of witnesses and arguments on the admissibility of the confession had added to its duration. On this Saturday alone, a total of twenty-two witnesses were heard from before the evidence was noted closed.

Despite the lateness of the afternoon and the fact that a full slate of witnesses had been before the Court, a *Telegram* reporter thought, "Interest in the case is very great, and the crowd in attendance is large."[7] Hartley Dewart asked that the trial be continued on the following Monday, a day when the prosecution could call on the great B.B. Osler to deliver its summation. For their part, Johnston and Murdoch felt that the momentum was with them and they urged that the case proceed. Chancellor Boyd decided to leave it up to the jury and after a short conference they asked that the trial continue.

As Clara had testified, the defence was obliged to go first and at three o'clock that afternoon Blackie Johnston rose to address the jury on behalf of his client.[8] In an era when forensic science was still in its infancy, the power of the advocate to sway a jury was still a crucial factor in any criminal trial. In the absence of DNA tests, fingerprinting or video surveillance, it was the words of the advocate that frequently made all the difference between guilt or innocence. Johnston began slowly, astutely reminding the jurors that he had not taken this case expecting any payment at all but simply because he believed Clara Ford to be innocent of murder. There was no halfway verdict here, he warned them. Either Clara was guilty of murder or she was not.

Then he began to wade into the Crown's case. He cautioned the jurors that they had come to the courtroom with "detectives and jail birds." Libby Black, currently serving her third jail term for public drunkenness, was a perjurer and not a credible witness. Was this the best the Crown could do, "ransack the moral sewers of the city to rake up evidence against the prisoner?" They had Frank Westwood's *ante-mortem* statement made "on the border between time and eternity" in which he had declared that the assassin was a medium-sized man with a moustache. Johnston gestured towards the prisoner's dock and asked if this could possibly apply towards the accused? "Do you mean to say," asked Johnston, "that with the light shining in the hall, he could not tell whether it was a Negro or a white man who stood on the steps?"

As for the letters of 1890 which linked Clara to Frank, he reminded the jury that at that time Clara was 28 while Frank was a lad of 14. "What could have been between them?" he asked. What indeed. The letters clearly showed that they knew each other. Yet Johnston's approach was an ingenious one, a line of argument that defended not only his client, but the spirit of the dead boy. Clara and Frank had not been lovers and had not even known each other. "It was unworthy of the Crown," he sniffed, "to attempt to vilify the character of the dead youth by advancing the motive they had." The jury would exonerate both Frank and Clara if they agreed with the defence's theory that they had not been lovers, had not known each other and that there was no attempted rape. It would be a most satisfactory conclusion and would foster respectability among all concerned.

Then it was the turn of the police.

From four o'clock until eleven thirty the police with Reburn had confined her, "as she had so tersely put it, digging at her for seven long hours."9 Is it not likely, Johnston asked the jurors, "that she, womanlike, would say anything to get out of the clutches of these vultures?" Johnston said little about Inspector Stark, a highly esteemed figure in Toronto society, and appreciated that a general attack on the police was unlikely to succeed. He conceded that Stark was, "not so much to blame" (even though his client had accused him of inventing the details of her confession) and that Porter and Slemin were "reasonably fair." Johnston concentrated his venom on the main interrogator. Sergeant Reburn was the "skilled, experienced, relentless, merciless officer..." who had extracted a confession from an innocent female. Under Johnston's beguiling hand, Reburn became the real accused. This same officer who had urged Clara to take her case to the jury and who had helped her to hire a lawyer, became the villain. This was a case of an unscrupulous man with a hapless woman at his mercy. "Because he [Reburn] had a woman to deal with he thought he could tire her out, and make a reputation on her conviction." At times, Johnston's use of violent hyperbole, his shower of obloquy, seemed to transcend the era's legal etiquette. Not only was Reburn a ruthless cross-examiner, he had subjected Clara "to such brutal, inhuman treatment; it made the learned counsel ashamed to be a man, to belong to the same race of beings." It was a mark of Johnston's intuitive genius to present an argument that while it had only the thinnest veneer of legality, nonetheless played heavily to the public's sympathy for the poor, lone woman and its dread of an overbearing police power.

Johnston reminded the jury that other than the disputed confession, there was no real evidence against Clara. The bullet evidence had demonstrated nothing. The jury should put aside the so-called confession and instead consider Clara's demeanour in the stand.

Clara Ford on trial, Toronto News, *May 1, 1895.*

Even with her life at stake, she had willingly entered the box, "to tell her story. She had taken the stand in one of the boldest, noblest, and most heroic acts ever witnessed in a criminal court in this land." He asked the jury to contrast her gallant conduct with that of the police. Lastly, he made a "fervid appeal for his client's life as a protest against the autocratic and czar-like action of the detectives in the cells." Nearing the end of two and a half hours of rhetorical fireworks, Johnston closed by reminding the jury of their awesome choice. "Think of the terrible responsibility if you make a mistake on the evidence. Think of the poor lone Negro girl, weigh the evidence and render your verdict accordingly. Give me her life," he begged them, "take it away from the hangman and give it to me."

It was an impressive appeal to the emotions that steered clear of most of the facts and instead emphasized the prisoner's sex, race and the opportunity for the jury to make this case a "protest" against the police and their "czar-like" tactics. It had little to do with the events of the night of October 6, 1894 and everything to do with who was virtuous and who was not.

Hartley Dewart, a perennial supporting counsel, was suddenly thrust into the uncomfortable role of presenting the Crown's case in one of the most public trials in Canada's history. He began modestly enough by announcing that this was a case "for an abler counsel than himself" but that he would lay out the facts as best he could.

Going directly to Johnston's accusations against the police, Dewart maintained, "It has become a common thing for the detectives to be slandered. They acted in a proper manner, for they detained the prisoner until they investigated the charge of murder against her." The central issue was whether or not the confession was true. Dewart went to the heart of the matter, that while the defence had condemned the police tactics, they had stopped short of actually accusing the detectives of perjury. "Well, what in God's name is it?" he asked. "Look at the confession, gentlemen, look at the way in which it was given. It was not wrung from her." The confession was the keystone of the Crown's case for "If you believe that Clara Ford confessed she shot Frank Westwood, it is your legal, your moral, your bounden duty to find her guilty." He reminded the jurors that if the confession was improperly admitted that this was a legal issue and would be rectified by the Court of Appeal where "everything will be done to protect the interests of the prisoner."

While Johnston had struck a strident, emotional tone, Dewart followed a course much closer to the facts. As for the alibi evidence, Dewart asked the jury to dismiss it completely. Mrs. Dorsay had an atrocious memory and she was clearly intent on assisting her friend. The other alibi witnesses were vague or unreliable. The only evidence which had been taken down at the time of the murder and which had been maintained consistently ever since was that of Flora McKay and the Croziers. This evidence, from the accused's putative daughter and her friends was in direct, hopeless contradiction to Clara's sworn testimony. Dewart asked the jurors to see subtle omissions by the defence. They had made no real attempt to question

Flora, and he asked, "Is there any reason why the putative child of the prisoner should tell a story which tells so strongly against her mother?" They had not questioned her because she was telling the truth and nothing they asked could have shaken her. If anything, Flora had manifested a desire to help Clara in any way she could and this made her testimony all the more damning. In total, Clara had contradicted thirteen witnesses on material points. Nine of these witnesses were impartial and the other four were police officers. "What can you conclude," Dewart implored the jury, "but that her statement was a bold and unblushing perjury."

Next, Dewart took the jurors through Clara's claim that the Toronto police had persecuted her. She alleged that they had tormented her for hours until at last she said what they wanted to hear. Dewart asked the jury to contrast this story with Clara's performance on the witness stand where she had been bold, self-confident and had defended herself on cross-examination with great fortitude. Not only was she anything but a defenseless waif, she had described in "marvellous minuteness" what had occurred in the detectives' office. Yet, never in the six months since the confession had there been a word in public alleging that the police had mistreated her. Turning the table on the defence lawyers, Dewart pointed out the strange coincidence between Clara's new story and the defence's position. "I ask you to recollect the manner in which Clara Ford spoke of the detectives. Did you note the legal mind? Did you not observe its counterpart in the address to the jury by the learned counsel for the prisoner?" Dewart's insinuations could not have been more pointed. He felt that it was apparent that her lawyers had deliberately concocted Clara's story of being pressured by the police. They had coached her on the details and how to present her yarn so that it fit into the main case that the police were the real culprits. It was a malicious assault on the integrity of Johnston and Murdoch, but given the savagery of their attacks on the police, there was little give and take left between the warring sides.

Finally, Dewart turned to Clara's demeanour on the witness stand. Yes, she had shown great courage but, "Was it not the courage that comes from a spirit of bravado?" he asked. While the jurors may have admired this bravado, "is it the admiration that you have for the daring or recklessness of the Mexican bandit or the admiration of the Indian stoic, who knowing no fear would go so far as to shoot down a man, though he knew his life might pay the penalty the next moment?" He did not deny that Clara had exhibited a spirit of reckless bravery but asked whether this was consistent with true innocence.

Dewart closed his summation. Despite his modesty, he had given a worthy performance, and the evidence against the prisoner had been fairly and eloquently put to the jury. Chancellor Boyd adjourned the Court for dinner. The judge would then give his summation and leave Clara's fate to the twelve jurors.

CHAPTER FOURTEEN

Cheers In Court

Gaslight and shadow played across the faces in the Adelaide Street Courthouse when Chancellor Boyd reconvened the Court at eight o'clock that evening. Two gas jets above the judge's bench illuminated the front of the chamber while a chandelier cast a glow across the body of the courtroom. A *Telegram* reporter described the scene where Clara sat "motionless as ever, her dark eyes turning alternatively from the judge to the jury."[1] The light of the chandelier failed to penetrate the broad brim of her hat and kept most of her face in shadow. In front of her, at the lawyer's benches, Johnston, Murdoch, Dewart and Curry shuffled their papers. As they had done during the course of the trial, Detectives Porter and Slemin sat behind the Crown lawyers. Also behind the prosecution sat Benjamin Westwood, patiently listening to the summations and occasionally reaching out to grasp the wooden railing before him. Despite the fact that it was eight o'clock on a Saturday night, the courtroom was as packed as ever.

The Clara Ford trial was apparently the best show in town and those who could not wedge themselves into the courtroom stood outside in the halls or milled around the Court precincts. A writer for the *Star* observed that word had gone around the city that the trial was nearing its climax and, "inside the (courthouse) corridors the staircases and some of the private offices were packed with people eagerly discussing the sensational features of the trial."[2] The *Telegram* reporter noted that as they waited for the judge's charge, "Every face in the room was upturned with eager intentness and the whole scene was an opportunity for a Hogarth."

Before the case went to the jury there was a final judicial ritual to be observed. Boyd would charge the jury, explaining the relevant law, advising them of the burden of proof and assisting them in their determination of the facts by going through the evidence.[3] It was also one of the judge's roles to explain the various theories of the prosecution and the defence. While the judge had a right to express his own views on credibility or the weight of various pieces of evidence, he must make it clear that issues of fact were strictly the domain of the jury. Still, given the eminence of the judge, it must have seemed that his words would carry great authority.

He began, fairly enough, by asking, "Has the crime been brought to the prisoner?" In answering the question, they were to set aside sympathy or compassion and be guided solely by the evidence. As far as that evidence disclosed, both the prisoner and the deceased were of good character. Boyd wished to steer clear of any unpleasant character issues so as to spare the Westwood family any further suffering. Still, he was obliged to note that it was a moot point if Frank had assaulted Clara or not. "A great many young men are very good at home and different away." The *ante-mortem* statement indicated that a moustached man of medium height had shot Frank. The jurors were to judge if this statement exonerated Clara. This point led into a discussion of the disputed confession and the chancellor visibly

Clara Ford awaits her verdict, Toronto Globe, *May 2, 1895.*

warmed up when he addressed this central point. They had heard much about the police, but he cautioned the jury, "If we had no crime in this country we would not need these officials, but so long as we have crime we must have detectives." Just as much as the judges and the courts, the police were a vital aspect of public safety. If the police had acted as the defence suggested, then, "They are not only unworthy of their position and false to their trust but they deserve to be behind prison bars." But he reminded the jurors that these were long service officers with sterling records. With that in mind, just who was likely to be telling the truth about what had happened in the detective's offices that night?

Boyd then dealt with a few issues that resonated with him. Clara had testified that she did not know Frank Westwood. Yet there was evidence that she had told Mrs. Crozier that she had known him since he was a boy. In Boyd's opinion, the testimony of the Crozier family was all-important. They had nothing against Clara and if anything were her closest friends. Their testimony was therefore bound to be reliable, as close to a true recitation of the facts as the jury would ever get; and the evidence of the Croziers was that Clara was at their house till late that Saturday night. She appeared to be excited (or drunk) and was carrying a revolver. This evidence was completely irreconcilable with the story Clara had given on the stand. As well, Flora McKay, "who gave her evidence with apparent truthfulness and candor," swore that she was not with Clara that night and further that Clara had asked her to lie about this fact.

Turning to the most dramatic evidence given during the trial, Boyd referred to Clara's performance in the witness box. He instructed the jury to disregard any notion of her "heroic conduct." Waxing biblical, he reminded the jurors of the passage in the Book of Job, "Skin for skin. Yea, all that a man hath will he give for his life." That is, with her life at stake it was neither unusual nor particularly heroic that an accused person would go into the stand and relate a story that exonerated them. The underpinning of her defence was that she was a casualty of the police sweatbox. Boyd asked the jurors, "Is this prisoner a woman to be awed by the questions of detectives, or is she on the other hand, not a woman who could make up a story of this kind?"

To support Clara there was, admittedly, some alibi evidence. Mrs. Dorsay was prepared to swear that Clara had come home by eleven o'clock. All of the other evidence was to the effect that the outer doors were open till at least midnight, which was ample time for her to have returned from Parkdale. With regard to the *Telegram's* articles on high water at the lakefront, Boyd dismissed them as inconclusive for "a person such as the slayer of Westwood would not hesitate about rushing through water or even taking off her shoes." As had the Crown attorney, Boyd reminded the jury that Clara's testimony contradicted numerous witnesses, many of whom were friendly to her. It was a charge that the *World* considered "a fair presentation of the facts adduced, the charge was probably the strongest ever delivered against a prisoner in a court of justice."

It was also a strange address for what it omitted. At no time had the judge explained the concept of the onus of proof: that is that the Crown had to establish guilt beyond a reasonable doubt. This was central to any criminal trial and Boyd had simply forgotten to deal with it. As well, the defence had a right to have its theories put to the jury and Boyd had also neglected to do this. The trial judge's one important function in these situations was to give the jury address and Boyd's lack of experience in criminal matters was painfully exposed. Blackie Johnston rose and asked the judge to reconsider his address and bring the jury back to have all of the above issues explained to them. He also corrected the judge's understanding of the facts. In addition to Mrs. Dorsay, Eliza Reid had also sworn that she saw Clara return at eleven o'clock. Graham, the ticket man had testified that balcony seats were only sold on Saturday, the same day he had noticed Clara Ford in attendance. None of these facts had been brought to the jury's attention. Somewhat chagrined, the judge ordered that the jury be brought back to the courtroom and he corrected himself on these points. It was a good omen for the defence that the last admonition that the jury would hear from the judge was, "If on the whole of the evidence you are unsatisfied, you must acquit, gentlemen; the prisoner gets the benefit of the doubt." Finally, a few minutes before nine o'clock, the jury retired to consider their verdict.

Clara Ford's fate was now in the hands of John Cobbett, carriage builder from Yonge Street; Joseph Pollock, a weaver from Markham; Martin Grant, a blacksmith from Newmarket, and nine other men of similar background. They were asked to perform a task that none of them had done before and that they were unlikely ever to do again. It was their function to sort through the conflicting evidence, through the rhetoric and bluster of the past five days, and determine the truth of the matter. The great English jurist Sir William Blackstone had once boasted that the jury was a uniquely British contribution to world civilization. "Trial by jury," he maintained, "ever has been, and I trust ever will be looked upon as the glory of the English law."4 Glorious it may have been, but it also required men with no legal training or experience in the evaluation of complex evidence to separate truth from bluster. It was a process eminently subject to human frailty.

No sooner had the jurors trooped out than the constables finally lost control of the crowd. A din of conversation arose across the courtroom and grew in volume as knots of spectators joined to debate the merits of the prosecution or the defence. "Little groups all over the court room laughed and chatted, as if it was between the acts of a comedy," wrote the *Star's* reporter, "and sometimes one member of a coterie would glance in the direction of the prisoner, note her hopeless demeanor and the little group would become quiet."5 A *Globe* reporter chatted with a cluster of spectators who felt that the judge's charge was so strongly against Clara that there would either be a quick conviction or a drawn out debate among those few diehards who would hold out for her innocence. Johnston, not anticipating an early verdict, left Murdoch in charge at the defence table. Behind the prisoner's dock, Benjamin Westwood sat silently with folded arms, his head slightly bowed and oblivious to the noise. Occasionally, members of the public glanced at the prisoner who sat as stoic and motionless as she had through most of the trial. Clara did not even glance up as the clock turned past 9:00 and then 9:30. Then just before 10 o'clock, barely an hour into their deliberations, the foreman announced that the jury had reached a verdict. In a few tension-filled minutes, the jurors shuffled back into the courtroom and resumed their seats.

"How say you as to the prisoner at the bar?" the court clerk asked the foreman, "is she guilty or not guilty?"

"Not guilty," he replied.

A cheer began among the standees at the back of the Court. It

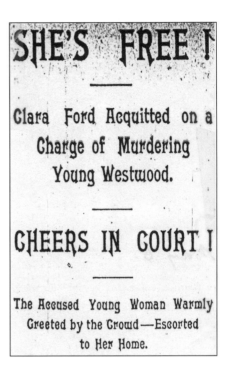

The jury finds Clara Ford "not guilty," Toronto News, *May 6, 1895.*

gained volume and intensity as it travelled forward until there was raucous applause throughout the room. Boyd sat quietly entering the verdict in his notebook and making no effort to quell the demonstration. When the din finally ceased, the clerk asked in the antiquated English of the courtroom, "Gentlemen of the jury, hearken to your verdict as the Court records it. You say the prisoner at the bar is not guilty, and that is the verdict of you all?" Several jurors nodded their heads and others simply said, "Yes." Cheers broke out again. Clara Ford sank back into the dock with a heavy sigh. As the plaudits of the crowd burst around her, she finally began to smile and glance around at her supporters. Chancellor Boyd ordered her to stand.

"Clara Ford, the jury has acquitted you of the crime with which you were charged. I am not surprised at the result, and for your sake I am glad. I am not sorry at the verdict, as it has cleared your character and also the character of the poor young fellow who is dead. Let me say one word more: Be kind to the little girl Florence McKay, who has shown her love for you though she was compelled to testify against you. I ask you to be kind to her, treat her gently and lovingly. You are free."

She responded with a simple "Thank you, sir" and stepped from the dock a free woman.

There was a universe of meanings in Boyd's simple admonition. Why was the judge not surprised at the jury's verdict, one that was so perverse to the evidence? Perhaps he realized that their sympathies would overwhelmingly be in favour of the poor Black woman who was allegedly so roughly handled by the police. Perhaps he suspected that some jurors believed her first story that she had been "insulted" by Frank Westwood and was only protecting her honour. Whatever the reason, Boyd seemed to accept it as human nature, a triumph of emotion over logic. Above all, it was an eminently convenient verdict, one that exonerated all concerned for it meant that Clara was not a murderer and that Frank was not a rapist.

To the crowd, the acquittal was the cause for euphoric celebration and Clara's partisans cheered with unrestrained exuberance.[6] The prisoner's dock became "a scene of the wildest tumult. Men fairly climbed over each other to shake hands with the woman who had just been acquitted." This crush of worshipful men had once again confined Clara to the prisoner's dock. Hastily she tried shaking with both hands to disperse her multitude of well-wishers. Pushing through the crowd was the waitress Eliza Reid. Upon reaching Clara she threw her arms around her and kissed her repeatedly. Eliza then took the vindicated woman in her arms and tried to steer her out of the courtroom. But no sooner had Eliza gotten her outside than Clara became the property of the mob. Hoisted upon male shoulders, she was carried in triumph through the streets of downtown Toronto and despite the hour hundreds of people watched or took part in this remarkable procession. At one point the parade halted so that Clara could be shown a late edition of the *Star* with a headline proclaiming her innocence. Perched on men's shoulders, she read the "glad headline" under the glare of an electric lamp. A few minutes later the other city dailies were issuing late editions announcing the same news.

There is no record of either Clara or Benjamin Westwood's reaction to the verdict.

At last the procession ended at Mrs. Dorsay's restaurant where Clara presided over an impromptu banquet. The crowd had tried to follow into the limited space at Mrs. Dorsay's and it took the redoubtable landlady some time to convince them that only a few intimates could stay before she could bolt the door. Once inside and savouring her freedom, Clara chatted with a reporter from the *Telegram*. She expressed her thanks to him and to that newspaper for its consistent editorial support, "The *Telegram* was the only paper that was fair." The reporter then asked what she planned to do. "Well, I don't intend to starve," Clara responded, ""I'm not that kind of a woman. I'd shovel coal first." Mrs. Dorsay petted her affectionately on the shoulder and added, "The good Lord was in it. I prayed to him and He helped Clara."

Still, the crowd on the street wanted more and Clara was called to the window to address them. "I thank you for the way you stood by me" she called out, "this does the boys of Toronto great credit."

The party continued on into the following day as groups of supporters, or the curious, gathered at Mrs. Dorsay's to see the famous Clara Ford. Among her well-wishers was the jury foreman, along with several other jurors.

CHAPTER FIFTEEN

Triumph

It did not appear to trouble the men who carried Clara through the Toronto streets in this surreal triumphal parade that they were celebrating the release of a woman who was the admitted killer of an eighteen-year-old boy. There can be no serious doubt that Clara Ford murdered Frank Westwood. Her confession was detailed and clear and there was no credible evidence that it had been coerced. That she perjured herself during her "heroic" appearance in the witness box is glaringly apparent from the numerous contradictions between her testimony and that of nearly every other witness. Had she been a man, it is almost certain that she would have been convicted and gone to the gallows.

Yet she was not a man and this made all the difference. A *World* reporter contacted a number of the jurors and found that even after Boyd's summation in which he had leaned so heavily in favour of guilt that the jury still stood nine to three for acquittal. The majority took less than an hour to convince the other three to come around. After discussions with the jurors, the reporter found that they were motivated by a sentiment "very deep-seated and very general in the hearts of men, is that which revolts from the capital execution of women" for there were "very few men so little touched by sentiment as not to shrink from the idea of hanging a woman."[1] The *World* reporter also discovered that by and large the jurors had accepted the defence's position that Clara had been a victim of the "dreadful institution," the sweatbox. The fact that so many of the jurors would publicly celebrate Clara's acquittal was remarkable in itself. Chancellor Boyd was later reported to have soundly deplored this jury's conduct and that this was "the most disgusting example of the weakness of the jury system he recalled in his long experience."[2]

Was it weakness, or was it motivated by the sense of "chivalry" which still motivated so many 19th century juries? Chivalry, originally derived from medieval codes of manners, continued to dominate male perceptions of how women should be treated.[3] Chivalry viewed the female as a delicate, vulnerable creature, whom men were supposed to venerate and protect. It was difficult for a Toronto gentleman to conceive that such a gentle creature could stalk and kill an able-bodied man. Women were to be protected, not prosecuted. Could a jury of men "Take that woman to the executioner?" The question was posed, not by Johnston, but by B.B. Osler in the murder trial of Maria Hartley in 1894.[4] The similarity in rhetorical style to that employed by Johnston on behalf of Clara Ford is striking. Both lawyers stressed their client's femininity and the juror's horror of sending a woman to the gallows. These notions of chivalry obviously applied to a respectable white lady. But could this reverence be extended to a more marginal member of society such as Clara Ford?[5]

Apparently it could; sex was more persuasive factor than class. Only a few weeks before the Clara Ford trial, an English jury had considered the case of Amy Gregory, a poor laundress who had strangled her six-week-old baby.[6] Much as in the case of Clara Ford, there was immense sympathy for her because she was poor and female. The *Spectator* felt that this sympathy was based on an assumption, "that women, from natural deficiency of reasoning power and natural liability to obey impulse, are partially irresponsible, or at least less responsible than men are." That her poverty might even be considered as partially excusing her conduct was apparent when the *News* expressed its chivalric euphoria in its post-trial editorial when it described the rescue of this "friendless girl, who has been subject to persecution all her life." Blackie Johnston had alluded to the pressing need for chivalry and the inability of women to think clearly when he reminded the jury of his client's vulnerability, "was it any wonder that she *womanlike* (emphasis added) would say anything to get out of the hands of these vultures." The imputation was that a man would have acted rationally a woman would not. Whether chivalry was based on the high regard for women, sympathy for their powerlessness or consideration of their diminished mental capacities, it was a potent force and was most apparent at the wild celebration of Clara's acquittal by what seems to have been an overwhelmingly male crowd. Chivalry had prevailed; the boys of Toronto had come through.

Of course, chivalry had its price. "Women have many traits in common with children...," wrote the criminologists Cesare Lombroso and William Ferrero in 1900, "their moral sense is deficient."[7] Women could be excused their faults more easily than men because of their childlike nature. However, the double standard in justice was bound to be matched by a double standard in society. It meant that women were unfit for the professions, for higher paying labouring jobs or to take part in public life. The same system that kept Clara Ford in grinding poverty had, on this occasion, saved her life.

Even if the jury's decision was hopelessly at odds with the evidence before it, it was not unheard of, then or now, for a jury to render an acquittal in the face of apparent guilt. Eighty years later, in the Morgentaler case, a jury would acquit a self-confessed abortionist in a verdict that was more a comment on the perceived inadequacy of the law. A legal commentator on the Morgentaler verdict thought that, "Unfairness, sympathy, dislike of harsh laws, disapproval of police or prosecution tactics they (the jury) may be told to ignore, but if they take them into consideration they are only speaking for the community as a whole."[8] The same comments could well be applied to the unusual results in the case of Clara Ford. It may also be the case that the jury was thereby giving its judgment on what they felt were heavy-handed police tactics.

Nor was Clara's acquittal the only time a jury would display chivalry to release a female murderer. In 1915, Carrie Davies, a Toronto servant, shot and killed her employer, Charles Massey.[9] Davies was a most compelling young lady, an immigrant who needed her menial job to send money back to her impoverished relatives in Britain. On one occasion, Massey had made lewd comments to her and later he attempted a sexual assault. Davies was torn between the need for her job and her loyalty to Mrs. Massey. In desperation, she shot Charles Massey on his own doorstep as he returned from his office. Ironically, she was defended by Hartley Dewart who this time had the pleasure of riding the wave of sympathy for the poor girl who was only trying to do her job and save her purity for her soldier sweetheart. Still, it was apparent that she was in no immediate danger and could simply have quit her job. Her act of murder was willful and without any urgent provocation. However when Carrie Davies' case went to the jury, Dewart reminded them that if she had been raped that, "she would have been a fallen woman, an outcast, one more sacrifice to brutish lust." To the *Star* the case was highly reminiscent of the Clara Ford affair for "It is now getting on 11 years (20 actually) since Toronto was stirred to its very depths by the Westwood crime."[10] Davies was a far more vulnerable

The News *portrayed the famous Clara Ford in male attire, Toronto* News, *Nov. 21, 1894.*

and sympathetic character than Clara Ford and it is not too surprising that she was also acquitted, for the *Star* went on to note, "The case of a woman charged with murder being treated with marked leniency, presumably on account of her sex is not altogether rare in the criminal annals of Ontario." Indeed, when serious crimes were at issue, it seemed to be the norm. Not long after this triumph, Dewart became a prominent figure in Ontario political life and in 1919 became leader of the provincial Liberals.

A few days after Clara's release there was a more sober assessment of what her acquittal meant for police morale and if anything the Toronto newspapers seemed to rally in support of the police force. The *Globe* led the way by reminding the public how effusive in their praise everyone had been when Clara Ford was first arrested and the mystery solved. There was certainly a "strong case of suspicion" against her, no matter what the jury ruled and no cause to criticize

Henry Reburn served a remarkable 46 years in police service, Toronto News, *Nov. 29, 1894.*

the detectives who, after all, "exist for the protection of the law-abiding public and to be a terror to evil-doers."[11] By any fair analysis, the police were quite right to arrest her and therefore the *Globe* editorialist asked, "in what particular did the officers overstep their duty?" The *Evening Star* also seconded this feeling for they wrote, "It would require no second thought to choose between detectives and crime." The *World's* writers continued to grumble about the outcome and turned their displeasure against the jurors who "had the bad taste to visit the prisoner at her house and congratulate her on her escape." To them, there was no doubt that the acquittal was an escape, not a vindication. The *Sentinel*, the organ of the provincial Orange Lodge, sanctimoniously noted that in due course, "the recording angel and justice such as only God can give" would be visited upon Clara Ford. For their part, the Toronto police expressed in a subtle way their disappointment at the result. In the chief constable's report for 1895, it was recorded that, "In the case of a woman who had confessed to the cold-blooded murder of a young man at his father's door the jury returned a verdict of acquittal." The addition of the phrase "who had confessed" expressed as fully as they could the police dismay that the palpably guilty had been freed.

Yet the acquittal did not seem to affect the careers of the officers involved. Inspector William Stark became deputy chief constable in 1906. At the time of his death in 1915 he was remembered and saluted for organizing Toronto's first effective detective department.[12] Charles Slemin, who had done much of the initial spade work in finding Clara, left Toronto and became chief constable of Brantford where he was awarded the Distinguished Service Medal in 1912. Henry Reburn moved from the Toronto force in 1904 to become an inspector for the Ontario Provincial Police and held this rank until his retirement in 1920. In all, Henry Reburn served a remarkable forty-six years in police service.

If the Ford acquittal was a passing embarrassment for the police, it was a major career boost for Blackie Johnston. It was a widely reported victory and it solidified his reputation as one of the finest defence lawyers in Canada. But it would be a mistake to consider his defence of Clara Ford to have been done purely in a spirit of self-promotion. In 1901, Johnston, assisted by T.C. Robinette, defended David Hawes, a Black railway porter who stood accused of raping a white girl at Union Station.[13] Despite the absence of any evidence of penetration or violence and despite Johnston's best efforts, Hawes was convicted and sentenced to ten years imprisonment. This case was in some respects the mirror image of Clara Ford's for the evidence against Hawes was weak. But the accusation of a Black man raping a white woman was so powerful that it was almost inevitable that a white male jury would convict. As the Toronto News felt, "He was lucky to have gotten away with a prison term. In the southern states he would have been lynched." The Hawes case also showed the sheer capriciousness of the jury system. The patently guilty Clara was freed while a Black man against whom there was only the thinnest sheen of evidence was considered lucky to have avoided lynching.

Nevertheless, in the face of great adversity and for no personal gain, Johnston had intensely struggled for Hawes's freedom. Over time, Johnston's criminal practice gave way to involvement in high-paying corporate affairs. By the time of his death in 1919, he was one of the most influential and wealthiest members of the Ontario bar.

After the crowds disbursed, two unresolved questions remained. The first was whether or not the confession should have been admitted into evidence. Chancellor Boyd had expressed the hope that a "stated case" to the Court of Appeal would result in a definitive opinion and guide the police as to what they could and could not do. However, Clara's acquittal left this unresolved. In following years, it seemed that the public came to accept the necessity of police interrogations as part of their investigations. Some grumbled about this perceived loss of civil liberties and in the *Canadian Bar Review* of 1929 one defence lawyer wrote that, "It must be self-evident to any person who attends a regular criminal assize that the large number of confessions which are classed a 'voluntary' have been extracted from prisoners by means of questioning and questioning and more questioning until sufficient evidence has, in the opinion of those interested, been obtained."[14] Despite his misgivings, Canadian courts were prepared to follow the 1914 British decision in Ibrahim that so long as a confession was voluntary and made without fear of prejudice or hope of advantage that it was admissible.[15] Since that time, it has become the case that, "The defining characteristic of the modern police interrogation is its almost universal endorsement by the policing community as a necessary component of any effective investigation."[16] In fact, the interrogation is now considered to be the crucial stage at which a suspect's fate is sealed. In retrospect, Boyd's decision to admit the confession was sound and consistent with principles on the admission of evidence.

The other unsettled problem was why did she kill? This is the question that still defies any satisfactory response. Was Clara the victim of a cruelty lodged where she could not forgive it? Although not flamboyantly evil, Clara's fragile self-restraint was tempted by some slight or some injury for which she could never forgive Frank Westwood. What that injury was remains the central mystery of the affair. Whether it was a clumsy attempt at rape or an adolescent comment on her mannish ways, it was enough to propel her (with the aid of a little whisky) to carry out the deed of October 6. Or was there some truth to the Crown's assertion that she loved Frank and had such an erotic infatuation that she could not stand the prospect of losing him? Despite their difference in age and race, it seems likely that they had known each other for years and had interacted on many occasions. When Frank proved unattainable, did she decide that no other woman would have him?

Whatever the motive, Clara had a huge investment in the Westwood tragedy and was determined to exploit it to the full. A reporter from the *News* interviewed her at Mrs. Dorsay's a few days after the trial. When asked about her plans she responded, "I hardly know what to do as yet. I have been offered work by several people at my trade and some gentlemen from the Musée have made an offer for me to go there."[17]

"I don't approve of that," interjected Mrs. Dorsay, "she oughtn't to go and exhibit herself nowise. Its unchristianlike and not in keeping with the scriptures." The landlady was still smarting from Boyd's recalling her to the witness stand to see if she could read. It was most insulting, she thought, and "He [Boyd] will come to some ignominious end! I predict it."

Meanwhile, Clara continued to mull over her options as admirer after admirer stopped by the unlikely little restaurant at 152 York Street. In a few days she did make up her mind and appeared at the Musée in a tableau of herself wearing a man's attire and carrying a revolver. Now the public at large could, upon the payment of a small fee, gaze upon the famous Clara Ford. Moore's Musée was renowned

Blackie Johnston in later life. His victory at the Clara Ford trial solidified his reputation as one of the finest defence lawyers in Canada. Courtesy of the Law Society Archives.

for its exotic entertainments, which laid emphasis on women and Blacks. Earlier in the year it had featured, "The Amazons" and "the matchless Colored Comiques." Clara's display was also a knowing mockery of the justice system and a tacit admission that she was the murderess. It was a display that the *World* felt, "threatens to disgrace our judicial administration by (her) appearing as a heroine in a dime museum."[18]

In some ways, the display was also a fascinating comment on male sexual fantasies in the 1890s.[19] European and American aesthetes were developing avant-garde themes centred on powerful women who could dominate and emasculate men. By the late 19th century, artistic renderings of Salome displayed her outward purity and inward lust for revenge and violence. Drawings and sculptures of Delilah showed her as a strong, imperious woman in charge of the man and able to take his life at her pleasure. In a more popular way, Clara Ford gave vent to these same feelings of the powerful self-possessed woman able to control or destroy men at her whim.

One man who was definitely not amused by this display, avant-garde or not, was Blackie Johnston. He had Clara called into his office where he gave her a dressing down and reminded her that but for him she would have been convicted and faced the prospect of the gallows. He further suggested, "if there were any remnants of decency left in her she would immediately leave Canada." Apparently she did so for shortly thereafter there are no further references to her in the Toronto municipal directories. For a brief moment she had floated on the shoulders of the exhilarated crowd and then was heard no more. Interestingly enough, Johnston's chastisement also seems to be an acknowledgment of her guilt. However, it may not have been the end of Clara's notoriety for it was rumored that she had crossed the border and become an actress in a unique performing group, "Sam T. Jack's Creoles," the first troupe of performing Black females. It was understood that her act consisted of "a damsel who had killed a man in pursuance of the 'unwritten law.' "[20] If so, she had completed the transition from a dark seat in the balcony to where she had always wanted to be, a place in front of the footlights.

For their part, the Westwood family shunned notoriety and endured as one of the quietly respectable families of Toronto. Benjamin Westwood remained at the head of his fishing tackle business until 1919. At his death in 1935, he was widely mourned and remembered as one of the founders of Trinity United Church on Bloor Street. He was, according to the *Globe* "one of the old school of Toronto's businessmen."[21] Clara Westwood died two years later. Lakeside Hall is long since gone and the area where it once stood is now part of a ramp for the Gardiner Expressway. Along with the mansion, that part of Parkdale south of the railway tracks has been obliterated to make way for the expressway. North of the railway, remnants of old Parkdale remain in a number of fine Victorian mansions. Still largely residential, Parkdale has declined and now the closely packed houses and apartments are troubled by high rates of crime and drug use making it seem a bit like the old Ward.

The Westwood mansion at the foot of Jameson Avenue may be gone, but where the front lawn existed is still a grassy park that faces onto Lake Ontario. Anyone standing on this lush green site can look out over the breakwater that tries to contain the lake's turbulent waves. On a windy day it still seems to invite the young to test its waters. This was the same view of white tipped waves and sails that Clara Westwood had as she cradled her dying son in her arms. In the few hours that remained to them, they lingered in Frank's room, watching the lake and talking gently of the things they loved until, at last, the light failed.

NOTES

Chapter 1: "Mother, I Am Shot"

1. The shooting of Frank Westwood on October 6, 1894, was extensively covered by all of Toronto's daily newspapers. See "It May be Murder" in the *Globe*, October 8, 1894, and "Called to the Door and Shot Down," *World* of the same day. The quotes that follow are taken from these accounts.

2. "There is a girl in it...," *Mail*, October 9, 1894, and *World* of the same day. The quotes that follow are taken from these accounts.

3. "... the detectives profess...," *Globe*, October 10, 1894.

Chapter 2: Inquest

1. Background on Frank Westwood's death and funeral, *Globe*, October 12, 1894.

2. For more information on the inquest, see W. Holdsworth, *History of English Law*, Vol. I (London: Methune, 1966) 84-5.

3. Information on the stonehookers taken from the *Telegram*, accounts at the time.

4. Evidence of Albert Peer, from the *Telegram*, October 30, 1894.

5. Background and quotes regarding the inquest, see *Globe*, October 15, 16, 24 and 30, 1894, and *World*, October 11, 24 and 30.

6. See "Hornberry's Statement," *Mail* and *Empire*, October 12, 1894, and *Globe*, October 16, 1894.

7. Isaac Anderson "had heard...," *Globe*, October 24, 1894.
8. "It was learned from a private source...," *News*, October 8, 1894.
9. "We fooled around...," and following quotes, see *World*, October 30, 1894.
10. For background on motive, see *Telegram*, October 9, 1894.
11. Sir Arthur Conan Doyle (1859-1930) was a Scottish novelist known for his creation of the detective Sherlock Holmes. See also Hector Charlesworth, *Candid Chronicles: Leaves from the Notebook of a Canadian Journalist* (Toronto: Macmillan, 1925) 242-3.
12. *World*, October 29, 1894.

Chapter 3: Queen City

1. For information on crime rates in Toronto, see Toronto Police Museum, *Annual Report of the Chief Constable*, for the years 1894 and 1895.
2. For additional information on William Howland, see Ron Sawatsky, "William Holmes Howland" in *Dictionary of Canadian Biography*, Vol. XII (Toronto: University of Toronto Press, 1990) 453-5. See also Desmond Morton, *Mayor Howland: The Citizens' Candidate* (Toronto: Hakkert, 1973) 98.
3. Regarding Staff Inspector Archibald's raid, see Desmond Morton, *Mayor Howland: The Citizens' Candidate* (Toronto: Hakkert, 1973) 98.
4. For the story on an eleven-year-old boy fined, see C.S. Clark, *Of Toronto the Good: A Social Study: The Queen City of Canada As It Is* (Montreal: Toronto Pub., 1898) 5.
5. For background on Toronto police, see Nicholas Rogers "Serving Toronto the Good: The Development of the Toronto Police Force, 1834-86" in Victor L. Russell (ed.), *Forging a Consensus: Historical Essays on Toronto* (Toronto: University of Toronto Press, 1984) 116-40.
6. Regarding Inspector William Stark, see obituary in the *Globe*, January 29, 1915.
7. Alphonse Bertillon was the chief of the Paris identification bureau. For background on Bertillon, see Greg Marquis, *Policing Canada's Century: A History of the Canadian Association of Chiefs of Police* (Toronto: University of Toronto Press/Osgoode Society, 1993) 122-138.
8. Nicholas Rogers, "Serving Toronto the Good: The Development of the Toronto Police Force 1834-86," in Victor L. Russell (ed.), *Forging a Consensus: Historical Essays on Toronto* (Toronto: University of Toronto Press, 1984) 116-40.

9. *World* criticizes police, December 11, 1893.

10. For sources of references to Sunday streetcars, see *Globe*, July 22, 1893; "The Great Car Contest," *Globe*, July 31, 1893; "Sunday in Toronto," *Globe*, August 14, 1893; "The Laws will be Strictly Enforced," *News*, July 13, 1894. On streetcars generally, see J.M.S. Careless, *Toronto to 1918: An Illustrated History* (Toronto: Lorimer, 1984) 138 and 147.

11. Benjamin Westwood obituary from *Globe*, January 5, 1935.

12. On the expansion of Toronto and annexation of Parkdale, see Careless, 109-12 and 124.

13. "How English is Toronto!" see G. Mercer Adam, *Toronto Old and New* (Toronto: Mail Printing Company, 1891) 42.

14. Information on "Moore's Musée" from *Globe*, September 29, 1894.

Chapter 4: "You Know My Color"

1. In 1885, Louis Riel led an armed uprising of Métis, Indians and white settlers and declared a provisional government for Western Canada. Troops from eastern Canada were sent to put down the rebellion.

2. Background information on Gus Clark and the police was taken from the *Mail*, November 21, 1894.

3. For more information on Charles Slemin and George Porter, see Toronto Police Museum, *Nominal and Descriptive Roll: Toronto Police Force*, 1895.

4. Information on the Ward (St. John's Ward) is from Barrie Dyster, "Captain Bob and the Noble Ward: Neighbourhood and Provincial Politics in Nineteenth-Century Toronto" in Victor L. Russell (ed.), *Forging a Consensus: Historical Essays on Toronto* (Toronto: University of Toronto Press, 1984) 87-115. See also J.M.S. Careless, "They (foreigners) had alien customs, conversed together incomprehensibly, crowded into run-down inner areas, most notably 'the Ward,' " 157.

5. Description of Clara Ford's arrest from the *Globe*, November 21, 1894.

6. The most detailed account given of the interrogation and arrest is from the *Empire*, November 27, 1894.

7. Headlines in the *Star*, November 21, 1894.

8. For more on the alleged rape, see *Globe*, November 24, 1894, in which the paper accepts her story: "He Made Improper Advances To Her." The same paper retracts the story on November 27, 1894: "...the fair course is to suspend judgment."

Chapter 5: A Complete Solution

1. Background information on Clara's decision to get a lawyer is from the *Empire*, November 29, 1894.
2. Descriptions of Clara's appearance are taken from *Globe*, November 22, 1894, and the *World*, November 29, 1894.
3. For more on Denison's Court, see Gene Howard Homel, "Denison's Law: Criminal Justice and the Police Court in Toronto, 1877-1921" in *Ontario History*, Vol. 73 (September 1981) 171-172.
4. "Clergymen, curates, law...," *World*, November 29, 1894.
5. Description of the second appearance in Police Court is recounted in detail in the *Empire*, November 29, 1894.
6. "Gradually her gaze...," *Telegram*, November 29, 1894.
7. For background information on Elizabeth Workman, see F. Murray Greenwood and Beverley Boissery, *Uncertain Justice: Canadian Women and Capital Punishment, 1754-1953* (Toronto: Dundurn Press, 2000) 141-60.
8. For more information on congratulations to the detectives, see Toronto Police Museum, *Annual Report of the Chief Constable* for the year 1894; and *Globe*, November 29, 1894; *Mail*, November 22, 1894.

Chapter 6: Clara

1. For information on Clara Ford's origins, see Library and Archives Canada (LAC), 1871 Census of Canada, St. John's Ward, No. 1 Division, page 62, the entry for Jessie McKay: underneath her is an entry for "Clara" age 7. Also see Toronto Public Library, Municipal Directories showing the Stow family at 331 Yonge Street and Martha Ford as matron of the public nursery. In the 1870s, Mrs. McKay lives at Beech Street and then Queen Street West, until settling on Gloucester Street in 1883. News accounts of Clara's origins are found in *Globe*, November 22, 1894; *Mail*, November 23, 1894. The most detailed account is contained in *World*, December 12, 1894.
2. For the John Hoskin account, see *World*, November 24, 1894.
3. Park Street School *News*, November 24, 1894.
4. For more on the Abbott family of Toronto, see Catherine Slaney, *Family Secrets: Crossing the Colour Line* (Toronto: Natural Heritage, 2003).
5. The leading reference on the Black experience in Canada remains Robin Winks, *The Blacks in Canada: A History* (2nd. ed.) (Montreal; Kingston: McGill-Queen's University Press, 1997) 245-7; on Blacks in

Toronto, see Daniel G. Hill, "Negroes in Toronto, 1793-1865" *Ontario History*, Vol. 55 (June 1963) 73-89; and Adrienne Shadd, Afua Cooper and Karolyn Smardz Frost, *The Underground Railroad: Next Stop, Toronto!* (Toronto: Natural Heritage, 2002) Chapter 2: "Blacks in Early Toronto"; and for more on Wilson Abbott, see Robin Winks, "Wilson Ruffin Abbott" in *Dictionary of Canadian Biography*, Vol. X (Toronto: University of Toronto Press, 1972) 3. For more background on Blacks in Ontario, see Linda Brown-Kubisch, *The Queen's Bush Settlement: Black Pioneers 1839-1865* (Toronto: Natural Heritage, 2004).

6. For Denison's view of people with African ancestry, see George T. Denison, *Recollections of a Police Magistrate* (Toronto: Musson Book Co., 1920) 39.

7. Clara Ford refers to herself as "Spanish," see the *Mail*, November 21, 1894.

8. For accounts of Clara Ford in New York, see *Telegram*, November 28, 1894,

9. Clara Ford in Chicago, *World*, November 22, 1894; repeated in *Star*, November 23, 1894.

10. For Clara Ford's relationship with the Clarks, see *World*, November 23, 1894.

11. "She was of a very violent...," *Globe*, November 21, 1894.

12. "She had an ungovernable temper...," *Mail*, November 21, 1894.

13. For the recollections of Benjamin Vise, see *World*, January 6, 1895.

14. "Complained to her...," *Globe*, November 22, 1894.

15. For Clara's relationship with Samuel Barnett, see *Mail*, November 21, 1894.

16. "Her character was above reproach...," *World*, November 21, 1894.

17. "She used to dress up...," *Mail*, November 21, 1894.

18. For background information on female dress see Thorstein Veblen, "The Theory of the Leisure Class (1899)," quoted in Aileen S. Kraditor, (ed.). *Up From the Pedestal: Selected Writings in the History of American Feminism* (Chicago: Quadrangle Books, 1968) 136. See also Catherine Smith and Cynthia Greig, *Women in Pants: Manly Maidens, Cowgirls, and Other Renegades* (New York: H.N. Abrams, 2003) 162.

19. For information on Tennessee Claflin see, Barbara Goldsmith, *Other Powers: The Age of Suffrage, Spiritualism and the Scandalous Victoria Woodhull* (New York: Knopf, 1998) 193-94.

20. For the account of women bicycling, see the *Telegram*, September 8, 1894.

21. The "blazing saddles" phenomenon is referred to in Linda Kealey (ed.), *A Not Unreasonable Claim: Women and Reform in Canada, 1880s-1920s*. (Toronto: Women's Press, 1979) 16.

22. On Vic Steinberg in a saloon, see *News*, January 7, 1895.

23. For the story of the "Transformation Scene," see *News*, April 8, 1895.

24. "A remarkable specimen...," *Mail*, November 22, 1894.

25. "Masquerading woman in Parkdale," referred to in the *Telegram*, November 21, 1894.

26. "She shot down...," *World*, November 22, 1894.

27. The *World* accuses Clara Ford of sexual perversion, November 23-24, 1894.

28. Richard von Krafft-Ebing, *Psychopathia Sexualis: A Medico-Forensic Study* (Pantheon reprint, N1953) 398.

29. For the Amedee Chatelle case, see *World*, October 29, 1894. The case is also referred to in Martin L. Friedland, *The Case of Valentine Shortis: A True Story of Crime and Politics in Canada* (Toronto: University of Toronto Press, 1986).

30. For R. v McNaghton 10 Cl. & F. 200 (1843) on the insanity defence in Canada, see W.C.J. Meredith, "Insanity as a Criminal Defence: A Conflict of Views" in *Canadian Bar Review*, Vol. 25 (1947) 251-5.

31. For the Alice Mitchell case, see Lisa Duggan, *Sapphic Slashers: Sex, Violence and American Modernity* (Durham, NC: Duke University Press, 2000).

32. "Whether the Westwood...," *World*, November 24, 1894.

Chapter 7: The Sweatbox

1. "Clara's dusky face...," *Star*, December 1, 1894.

2. "A vital stage in the process...," from James W. Williams, "Interrogating Justice: A Critical Analysis of Police Interrogation and Its Role in the Criminal Justice Process" in *Canadian Journal of Criminology*, Vol. 42 (April 2000) 209.

3. "The Truth is...," from Mark Bowden, "The Dark Art of Interrogation" in *The Atlantic*, Vol. 292 (October 2003) 51-69.

4. Crown Attorney Curry, "If I were counsel..." see *News*, November 29, 1894.

5. For Arthur Conan Doyle's comments on the Ford case, see *World*, November 29, 1894.

6. For James Knowles comments, see *News*, November 29, 1894.

7. Background on the Day case from *Queen v Day* (1890) 20 Ontario Reports 209.

8. For more detail on the *Telegram's* defence of Clara, see the edition dated December 1, 1894.

9. Taken from the Ottawa *Free Press*, as reported in the *News*, January 21, 1895.

10. Background on rapes in York County is from Carolyn Strange, "Patriarchy Modified: The Criminal Prosecution of Rape in York County, Ontario, 1880-1930" in Phillips, Loo and Lewthwaite (eds.), *Essays in the History of Canadian Law: Vol. V, Crime and Criminal Justice* (Toronto: University of Toronto Press/Osgoode Society, 1994) 207-212.

11. On the cult of domesticity, see Barbara Welter "The Cult of True Womanhood: 1820-1860," *American Quarterly*, 1966. Also see Deborah Gorham, *The Victorian Girl and the Feminine Ideal* (Bloomington, IN: Indiana University Press, 1982).

12. For more information on single working women in Toronto of the time period, see Carolyn Strange, *Toronto's Girl Problem: The Perils and Pleasures of the City, 1880-1930*. (Toronto: University of Toronto Press, 1995).

13. On infanticide, see Constance B. Backhouse, "Desperate Women and Compassionate Courts: Infanticide in Nineteenth Century Canada" in *University of Toronto Law Journal*, Vol. 34 (Fall 1984) 447-75.

14. "As she grew older...," from *World*, November 29, 1894.

15. "Lazy, improvident, docile...," from Allen P. Stouffer, "A 'restless child of change and accident': The Black Image in Nineteenth Century Ontario" in *Ontario History*, Vol. 76 (June 1984) 128-137.

16. For background on Ebenezer Forsyth Blackie Johnston, see Law Society Archives, and J. Kristin Bryson, "Ebenezer Forsyth Blackie Johnston" in *Dictionary of Canadian Biography*, Vol. XIV (Toronto: University of Toronto Press, 1998) 541-2. Also see "When defending a case...," in W. Stewart Wallace, *Murders and Mysteries: A Canadian Series* (Toronto: Macmillan of Canada, 1931; reprinted Westport, CT: Hyperion Press, 1975) 79.

Chapter 8: Revelations of an Improper Sort

1. For an account on the Globe building fire, see *News*, January 7, 1895.

2. For the story of fire at the Osgoodby Building, see *News*, January 11, 1895.

3. Copy of the true bill, Ontario Archives, RG 22-392-0-8619 #258, Crown Attorney Criminal Indictment File.

4. For background on the indictment, see *Telegram*, January 19, 1895, and *Globe*, January 19, 1895.

5. "As the case is…," from *Telegram*, January 22, 1895.

6. For information on the Adelaide Street Courthouse, see C. Pelham Mulvany, *Toronto: Past and Present: A Handbook to the City* (Toronto: W.E. Caiger, 1884) 52.

7. For background on John Alexander Boyd, see Peter G. Barton, "Sir John Alexander Boyd" in *Dictionary of Canadian Biography*, Vol. XIV (Toronto: University of Toronto Press, 1998) 126-8; and "The Last Chancellor of Ontario" in *The Canadian Law Times*, Vol. 36 (1916) 909-13; and W.H.C. Boyd, "The Last Chancellor" in *Law Society Gazette*, Vol. 15 (1981) 356-67.

8. More information can be found in Britton Bath Osler, see "Fire in Dundas," Dundas *True Banner*, February 19, 1874; for general information, see John Honsberger "B.B. Osler, Q.C., The First President " in *Law Society Gazette*, Vol. 20 (1986) 146-56. See also Patrick Brode, "Britton Bath Osler" in *Dictionary of Canadian Biography*, Vol. XIII (Toronto: University of Toronto Press, 1994) 795-6.

9. The Denham slaughter and Jack the Ripper, see L. Perry Curtis, Jr., *Jack the Ripper and the London Press* (New Haven, CT: Yale University Press, 2001). Also see Karen Halttunen, *Murder Most Foul: The Killer and the American Gothic Imagination* (Cambridge, MA: Harvard University Press, 1998).

10. For more information on Reginald Birchall, see *Globe,* arrest March 3, 1890, and trial September 22 to October 15, 1890.

11. "Lizzie Borden owed her life…," see Ann Jones, *Women Who Kill* (New York: Holt, Rinehart and Winston, 1980) 231.

12. On Maria Manning and Adelaide Bartlett, see Judith Knelman, *Twisting in the Wind: The Murderess and the English Press* (Toronto: University of Toronto Press, 1998).

13. On women in revenge melodramas, see Carolyn Strange, "Wounded Womanhood and Dead Men: Chivalry and the Trials of Clara Ford and Carrie Davies" in Franca Iacovetta and Mariana Valverde (eds.) *Gender Conflicts: New Essays in Women's History* (Toronto: University of Toronto Press, 1992) 149-67.

14. For B.B. Osler's opening address, see *Globe*, May 1, 1895.

15. "Certain relationship of an improper sort…," in *World*, May 1, 1895.

16 Examination of Benjamin Westwood, from the *Telegram*, May 1, 1895.

17. The article including the statement, "missile of death" from the *News*, May 1, 1895.

Chapter 9: The Crown's Case

1. "I'm glad I wasn't there...," from the *Telegram*, May 1, 1895.
2. "I believe anything...," Ibid, May 1, 1895.
3. "What did she [Clara] say," and the quotes following are taken from the *News*, May 1, 1895.
4. Johnston's objection, as described in the Hamilton *Spectator*, May 4, 1895.
5. Ibid, tests on bullets.
6. Description of court scene, *Telegram*, May 2, 1895.
7. For accounts of Libby Black's testimony, see *News*, May 2, 1895.
8. For more information on interracial marriages in the 1860s, see Allen P. Stouffer "A 'restless child of change and accident': The Black Image in Nineteenth Century Ontario" in *Ontario History*, Vol. 76 (June 1984) 128-37; David A. Hollinger, "Amalgamation and Hypodescent: The Question of Ethnoracial Mixture in the History of United States" in *American Historical Review*, Vol. 108 (December 2003) 1363.
9. On John Randolph, see the *Telegram*, May 6, 1886.
10. Cross-examination of Libby Black, see *World*, May 2, 1895; *News*, May 2, 1895.

Chapter 10: Confession

1. Description of the courtroom as reported in the *News*, May 2, 1895.
2. Quotes from the trial, "I said that she was not...," in Ontario Archives, Chancellor Sir John Boyd Benchbooks (hereinafter *Boyd Benchbooks*), RG 22-439-1-19 *R. v Ford*, 75.
3. "She was alone...," from the *Telegram*, May 2, 1895.
4. Chancellor Boyd's comments, "I don't see why...," from the *Star*, May 2, 1895.
5. Ibid, "Clara: There's no misleading you...."
6. "Did she go in front...," from the *Telegram*, May 3, 1895.
7. Ibid, "Didn't you tell Clara...."
8. "Did she tell you...," from the Hamilton *Spectator*, May 4, 1895.
9. Ibid, "Why was this woman kept...."
10. "The main facts of the story...," *Globe*, May 4, 1895.

Chapter 11: Ribbons and Bullets

1. Gus Clark's testimony, *Globe*, May 3, 1895.
2. Christian Dorenwend's testimony, *Telegram*, May 3, 1895.
3. "G. is a regular whore...," in *Boyd Benchbooks*, 9.
4. The quote " a severe shock to...," is taken from the Hamilton *Spectator*, May 4, 1895.
5. "Her conduct couldn't be...," from the *Telegram*, May 3, 1895.
6. Ibid, "I suppose you will see me...."
7. Information on William Elliott's testimony, from the *World*, May 4, 1895.
8. "The Crown's evidence...," from the *News*, May 3, 1895.
9. For more information on ballistics tests, see H.J. Walls, *Forensic Science: An Introduction to the Science of Crime Detection* (New York: Praeger, 1968) 166-7.
10. "The same little scratches...," from *Boyd Benchbooks*, 81.
11. Ibid, "I have seen plenty of such...."
12. "Not that the Westwood...," from the *World*, May 4, 1895.

Chapter 12: Clara's Version

1. The most detailed account of Clara's examination is taken from the *Globe*, May 4, 1895.
2. On Vic Steinberg, see *Telegram*, May 4, 1895.
3. Clara describes the Croziers, from the *World*, May 4, 1895.
4. Clara's testimony as performance, see Carolyn Strange, "Wounded Womanhood and Dead Men," 159.
5. "Clara if you don't...," from the *World*, May 4, 1895.
6. "In chief" is the term for when a witness is first asked questions by the lawyer who called the individual to the stand. The person is "examined in chief." When the witness is asked questions by the lawyer in opposition, this is called a cross-examination.
7. "Shaky ground if he...," from Carolyn Strange "Wounded Womanhood and Dead Men," 167.
8. "With the same jaunty...," from the *Globe*, May 4, 1895.
9. Commentary from the *World*, May 4, 1895.
10. Commentary from the *Telegram*, May 4, 1895.

Chapter 13: Final Battle

1. The "trial by newspaper" account is taken from the *News*, May 13, 1895.
2. Blackie Johnston protests against an article in the *World*, see the *Telegram*, May 4, 1895.
3. The reporters testify, *Telegram*, May 4, 1895.
4. Ibid, details of Chloe Dorsay's testimony.
5. Ibid, "Is Clara hot-tempered?"
6. Boyd notes Chloe Dorsay's comments, *Boyd Benchbooks*, 97.
7. "Interest in the case...," from the *Telegram*, May 6, 1895.
8. Details on Blackie Johnston's address to the jury, see the *Globe*, May 6, 1895.
9. Blackie Johnston's comments on the police, taken from the *Telegram*, May 6, 1895.

Chapter 14: Cheers In Court

1. Description of the courtroom, from the *Telegram*, May 6, 1895.
2. Courtroom description from the *Star*, May 6, 1895.
3. Details of Chancellor Boyd's summation from the Hamilton *Spectator*, May 8, 1895, and from the *Globe*, May 6, 1895.
4. On the jury system, see Glanville Williams, *The Proof of Guilt: A Study of the English Criminal Trial* (3rd ed.), (London: Stevens & Sons, 1963) 253-7.
5. "Little groups all...," from the *Star*, May 6, 1895.
6. Description of the celebration scene after verdict, see the *Globe*, May 6, 1895, and the *Telegram*, May 6, 1895.

Chapter 15: Triumph

1. "Very deep-seated...," from the *World*, May 6, 1895.
2. For Boyd's comments on the jury, see Hector Charlesworth *Candid Chronicles: Leaves from the Notebook of a Canadian Journalist* (Toronto: Macmillan, 1925) 244.
3. For background on chivalry, see Susan K. Datesman and Frank R. Scarpitti (eds.), *Women, Crime and Justice* (New York: Oxford University Press, 1980). Those who have studied women in the criminal justice system report that "women generally are treated more gently than men by officials at all levels of the system," 278. Also see Carol Smart, *Women, Crime and Criminology: A Feminist Critique*

(London: Routledge & K. Paul, 1977). "The overriding problem with much of the existing work on the discretion of the police and courts in their treatment of offenders is that it presumes the existence of an attitude of benevolence and chivalry on the part of law enforcement agencies towards female offenders," 138.

4. On B.B. Osler's comments, see *World*, October 29, 1894; *News* expresses its views on chivalry, May 6, 1895.

5. On the extension of chivalry to lower classes, see Carolyn Strange, "Wounded Womanhood and Dead Men," 151.

6. For the Amy Gregory case, see Judith Knelman, *Twisting in the Wind*, 155.

7. Regarding the price of chivalry, the view of women as children, see Cesare Lombroso and William Ferrero, *The Female Offender* (New York: Appleton, 1900) 151, quoted in Charalee F. Gray "Habilitation: Sentencing of Female Offenders" in *The Canadian Journal of Law and Jurisprudence*, Vol. 5 (January 1992) 121-122.

8. For the Morgentaler jury, see the editorial "Trial by Jury" in *The Criminal Law Quarterly*, Vol. 19 (December 1976) 1-2.

9. For more background on the Carrie Davies case, see Carolyn Strange, "Wounded Womanhood and Dead Men," for a thorough comparison of her case with Clara Ford's.

10. "It is now getting on...," from the *Star*, March 6, 1915.

11. Support for the police, see the *Globe* editorial, "exist for the protection...," May 9, 1895; the *Star* editorial May 9, 1895; the *World* editorial May 9, 1895; the *Sentinel* editorial May 9, 1895; and the Chief Constable's report for 1895, Toronto Police Museum.

12. For information on the careers of the police William Stark, see death, *Globe*, January 27, 1915; obituary, *Globe*, January 29, 1915. On Charles Slemin awarded DSM, see *Globe*, January 1, 1912; and Henry Reburn, obituary, *Star*, November 26, 1921.

13. On the David Hawes case, see Carolyn Strange, "Patriarchy Modified," 223-24.

14. "It must be self-evident...," from A.E. Popple "Questioning of Prisoners in Custody" in *Canadian Bar Review*, Vol. 7 (1929) 176-8.

15. *Ibrahim v. The King*, 1914, A.C. 599, followed in Canada by *Prosko v. The King*, 1922, 63 S.C.R., 226.

16. "The defining characteristic...," from James W. Williams, "Interrogating Justice: A Critical Analysis of the Police Interrogation and its Role in the Criminal Justice Process," in *Canadian Journal of Criminology*, Vol. 42 (April 2000) 209-214.

17. *News* interview, May 6, 1895.
18. Clara Ford at Moore's Musée, see the *World*, May 9, 1895.
19. For background on male sexual fantasies, see Bram Dijstra, *Idols of Perversity: Fantasies of Feminine Evil in Fin de Siecle Culture* (New York: Oxford University Press, 1986).
20. Regarding Clara Ford's later career, see Hector Charlesworth, *Candid Chronicles*, 244.
21. Obituary of Benjamin Westwood, *Globe*, January 5, 1935.

BIBLIOGRAPHY

Archival Material

Archives of Ontario: R.G. 22-439-1-19, Chancellor Sir John Boyd's
Benchbooks.
Library and Archives Canada: Census of 1871, St. John's Ward, No. 1
Division, p. 62.
Toronto Police Museum: *Annual Report of the Chief Constable* for the
years 1894 and 1895.
Nominal and Descriptive Roll, Toronto Police force, 1895.

Articles

Backhouse, Constance B., "Desperate Women and Compassionate
Courts: Infanticide in Nineteenth-Century Canada" in *University of
Toronto Law Journal,* Vol. 34 (Fall 1984) 447-75.
Barton, Peter G., "Sir John Alexander Boyd" in *Dictionary of Canadian
Biography,* Vol. XIV (Toronto: University of Toronto Press, 1998)
126-8.
Brode, Patrick, "Britton Bath Osler" in *Dictionary of Canadian Biography,*
Vol. XIII (Toronto: University of Toronto Press, 1994) 795-6.
Bryson, J. Kristin, "Ebenezer Forsyth Blackie Johnston" in *Dictionary of
Canadian Biography,* Vol. XIV (Toronto: University of Toronto Press,
1998) 541-2.

Dyster, Barrie, "Captain Bob and the Noble Ward: Neighbourhood and Provincial Politics in Nineteenth-Century Toronto" in Victor L. Russell (ed.), *Forging a Consensus: Historical Essays on Toronto* (Toronto: University of Toronto Press, 1984) 87-115.

Hill, Daniel G., "Negroes in Toronto, 1793-1865" in *Ontario History*, Vol. 55 (June 1963) 73-89.

Honsberger, John, "B.B. Osler Q.C., The First President" in *Law Society Gazette*, Vol. 20 (1986) 146-56.

Homel, Gene Howard, "Denison's Law: Criminal Justice and the Police Court in Toronto, 1877-1921" in *Ontario History*, Vol. 73 (September 1981) 171-86.

Popple, A.E., "Questioning of Prisoners in Custody" in *Canadian Bar Review*, Vol. 7 (1929) 176-8.

Rogers, Nicholas, "Serving Toronto the Good: The Development of the Toronto Police Force, 1834-86" in Victor L. Russell (ed.), *Forging a Consensus: Historical Essays on Toronto* (Toronto: University of Toronto Press, 1984) 116-40.

Sawatsky, Ron "William Holmes Howland" in *Dictionary of Canadian Biography*, Vol. XII (Toronto: University of Toronto Press, 1990) 453-5.

Stouffer, Allen P., "A 'restless child of change and accident': The Black Image in Nineteenth Century Ontario" in *Ontario History*, Vol. 76 (June 1984) 128-37.

Strange, Carolyn, "Patriarchy Modified: The Criminal Prosecution of Rapes in York County, Ontario 1880-1930" in Phillips, Loo and Lewthwaite (eds.), *Essays in the History of Canadian Law: Vol. V, Crime and Criminal Justice* (Toronto: University of Toronto Press/Osgoode Society, 1994) 207-51.

_____, "Wounded Womanhood and Dead Men: Chivalry and the Trials of Clara Ford and Carrie Davies" in Franca Iacovetta and Mariana Valverde (eds.), *Gender Conflicts: New Essays in Women's History* (Toronto: University of Toronto Press, 1992) 149-67.

Williams, James W., "Interrogating Justice: A Critical Analysis of the Police Interrogation and its Role in the Criminal Justice Process" in *Canadian Journal of Criminology*, Vol. 42 (April 2000) 209-14.

Books

Adam, G. Mercer, *Toronto Old and New* (Toronto: Mail Printing Company, 1891).

Careless, J.M.S., *Toronto to 1918: An Illustrated History* (Toronto: J. Lorimer, 1984).

Charlesworth, Hector, *Candid Chronicles: Leaves from the Notebook of a Canadian Journalist* (Toronto: Macmillan, 1925).

Clark, C.S., *Of Toronto the Good: A Social Study: The Queen City of Canada As It Is* (Montreal: Toronto Pub., 1898).

Datesman, Susan K. and Scarpitti, Frank R. (eds.), *Women, Crime and Justice* (New York: Oxford University Press, 1980).

Denison, George T., *Recollections of a Police Magistrate* (Toronto: Musson Book Co., 1920).

Dijstra, Bram, *Idols of Perversity: Fantasies of Feminine Evil in Fin de Siecle Culture* (New York: Oxford University Press, 1986).

Duggan Lisa, *Sapphic Slashers: Sex, Violence and American Modernity* (Durham, NC: Duke University Press, 2000).

Gorham, Deborah, *The Victorian Girl and the Feminine Ideal* (Bloomington, IN: Indiana University Press, 1982).

Greenwood, F. Murray and Boissery, Beverley, *Uncertain Justice: Canadian Women and Capital Punishment, 1754-1953* (Toronto: Dundurn Press, 2000).

Halttunen, Karen, *Murder Most Foul: The Killer and the American Gothic Imagination* (Cambridge, MA: Harvard University Press, 1998).

Jones, Ann, *Women Who Kill* (New York: Holt, Rinehart, and Winston, 1980).

Kealey, Linda (ed.), *A Not Unreasonable Claim: Women and Reform in Canada, 1880s-1920s* (Toronto: Women's Press, 1979).

Knelman, Judith, *Twisting in the Wind: The Murderess and the English Press* (Toronto: University of Toronto Press, 1998).

Kraditor, Aileen S. (ed.), *Up From the Pedestal: Selected Writings in the History of American Feminism* (Chicago, Quadrangle Books, 1968).

Marquis, Greg, *Policing Canada's Century: A History of the Canadian Association of Chiefs of Police* (Toronto: University of Toronto Press/Osgoode Society, 1993).

Morton, Desmond, *Mayor Howland: The Citizens' Candidate* (Toronto: Hakkert, 1973).

Mulvany, C. Pelham, *Toronto: Past and Present: A Handbook to the City* (Toronto: W.E. Caiger, 1884).

Shadd, Adrienne, Cooper, Afua and Smardz Frost, Karolyn, *The Underground Railroad: Next Stop, Toronto!* (Toronto: Natural Heritage, 2002).

Smart, Carol, *Women, Crime and Criminology: A Feminist Critique* (London: Routledge & K. Paul, 1977).

Smith, Catherine and Greig, Cynthia, *Women in Pants: Manly Maidens, Cowgirls, and Other Renegades* (New York: H.N. Abrams, 2003).

Strange, Carolyn, *Toronto's Girl Problem: The Perils and Pleasures of the City, 1880-1930* (Toronto: University of Toronto Press, 1995).

Wallace, Stewart W., *Murders and Mysteries: A Canadian Series* (Toronto: Macmillan of Canada, 1931; reprinted Westport, CT: Hyperion Press, 1975).

Walls, H.J., *Forensic Science: An Introduction to the Science of Crime Detection* (New York: Praeger, 1968).

Winks, Robin W., *The Blacks in Canada: A History*, 2nd ed. (Montreal; Kingston: McGill-Queen's University Press, 1997).

Newspapers

Hamilton *Evening Times*
Hamilton *Spectator*
Toronto *Empire*
Toronto *Globe*
Toronto *Mail*
Toronto *News*
Toronto *Star*
Toronto *Telegram*
Toronto *World*
Windsor *Evening Record*

INDEX

Abbott, Anderson Ruffin (Dr.), 47

Abbott, Wilson Ruffin, 46, 47

Adam, G. Mercer, 22

Adelaide Street Courthouse
(Toronto), 77, 93, 139

Allcock firm (UK), 22

Allcock, Leight and Westwood, 22

American Civil War, 46, 47, 94

Anderson, Isaac, 12

Archibald, David (Staff
Inspector), 17

Armour, Chief Justice, 66

Ballistics evidence, 108, 111-113

Baptist Church, 79

Barber, Minnie, 11

Barnett, Samuel, 26, 40, 51, 52,
108, 109, 116

Bartlett, Adelaide, 82

Beecher, Catharine, 70

Bennett, George, 127, 128

Benwell, Fred, 81

Bertillon system (forensics), 18

Birchall, ____ (Mrs.), 81

Birchall, Reginald, 81

Black, Libby (Mrs.), 93, 95, 97,
102, 122, 133

Black Crook, The, 23, 25, 27, 63,
89, 90, 123, 131

Black community (Toronto), 26,
27, 45-47, 50

Blackstone, William (Sir), 143

Bloom, Jennie, 110

Borden, Lizzie, 81

Boyd, John Alexander
(Chancellor), 23, 77-79, 90, 91,
97, 99, 107, 108, 112-114, 127,
129, 130, 132, 138-143, 145, 146,
148, 149, 155, 156

Brantford (ON), 154

Breslan, Jacob, 52

Canada Life, 75

Canadian Anti-Slavery Society, 47

Canadian Bar Review, 155

Canadian Pacific Railway, 79

Card, Ellen (Mrs.), 11

Cave, Justice, 66

Caven, John (Dr.), 9

Chatelle, Amedee, 60

Chatham (ON), 46

Chicago (IL), 48-50, 52, 123

Chivalry, see Women

Christie Brown bakeries
   (Toronto), 71

Clafin, Tennessee, 54

Clark, °°° (Mrs.), 49

Clark, Charles, 127

Clark, C.S., 18

Clark girls, 106, 107

Clark, Gus, 12-14, 24, 25, 37, 49,
   50, 52, 58, 90, 97, 106, 110, 123

Cobbett, John, 143

Cohen, Gussie, 110

Coleridge, Lord, 66

Collingwood (ON), 46

Coombes, °°° (Sergeant), 13

Cooper, Temple, 89

Confessions, rules of admission,
   98-100, 105, 113, 114, 121-123,
   132, 134, 136, 137, 140, 153

Criminal Code (1892), 73, 74
   Amendment, 74

Criminal insanity, 58

Crozier:
   Maggie, 29, 87-89, 101, 136
   Mary (Mrs.), 28, 29, 39-41, 63,
     87, 88, 98, 101, 115, 119, 122, 130,
     136, 141, 142
   Sadie, 89, 119

"Cult of True Womanhood, 1820-
   1860, The," 70

Curry, James Walker (Crown
   attorney), 4, 12, 18, 37, 39, 65,
   80, 108, 139

Davies, Carrie, 151

Day, Albert Hoyt, 66, 67, 73, 91, 99

Day, Desire (Mrs. A.H.), 66

Denham (England), 80

Denison, George T. (Colonel), 22,
   35-37, 42, 47, 103

De Tocqueville, Alexis, 94

Dewart, Hartley H. (Crown attorney), 8, 10, 11, 24, 80, 108, 113,
   122, 129, 132, 136-139, 151, 152

Dominion Medical Monthly, 55

Dorenwend, Christian, 106, 107

Dorsay boarding house, 69

Dorsay, Chloe (Mrs.), 27, 45, 48,
   52, 117, 128-132, 136, 142, 143, 147

Dorsay, Mame, 129, 131

Doyle, Arthur Conan (Sir), 14, 15,
   55, 65, 161

Elliott, William, 111-113

Emancipation Day, 23, 47

Empire, see Toronto newspapers

England, 82

Evening Record (Windsor), 53

Evening Times (Hamilton), 94

Exhibition Grounds (Toronto), 31,
   68, 69, 102, 103

Fall River (MA), 81

Fashion, women's dress, 53-55, 57

Ferrero, William, 150

Ford, Clara, ii, iii, 25-52, 54-56, 58-
   65, 67-74, 76-95, 97-124, 126-158
   arrest of, 32
   arraignment of, 35, 76, 78
   interrogation of, 27-32, 40
   origins of, 25, 44, 45, 115
   subsequent career, 156-158
   trial of, 77-80, 82-93, 95-146

Foundlings' Nursery (Toronto), 45

Free Press (Ottawa), 69
Fugitive Slave Act (1850), 46

Gardiner Expressway, 159
Gazette (Montreal), 69
Gladstone House (Toronto), 50
Globe (Toronto), see Toronto
  newspapers
Graham, William, 131, 143
Grand Opera (Toronto), see
  Opera House
Grant, Martin, 143
Grasett, H.J. (Chief Constable),
  16, 18, 42, 131
Great Britain, Britain, 22, 80, 81
Gregory, Amy, 149
Gurney's Foundry (Toronto), 30

Hart, ____ (Dr.), 3
Hart, ____ (Sergeant), 16
Hartley, Maria, 100, 149
Hawes, David, 154, 155
Home for Incurables (Toronto), 50
Homosexuality, 58, 59
Honour Killings, 82
Hornberry, W. Henry, 10, 14, 24
Hoskin, John, 45
Howland, William (Mayor), 17

Infanticide, 71, 72
Insanity defence, see also Chatelle,
  Amedee 60, 61, 74
Interracial marriage, 94, 110
Interrogation, techniques of, 63-
  65, 67-70, 155
Inquest, 7-16, 24, 52

Jack the Ripper, 80
Jacobs and Sparrow's Opera
  House (Toronto), 29

Jews community, in Toronto, 26,
  108
Jewish shops:
  Leovsky and Berman (butch-
    ers), 26
  Rabinowich (watchmaker), 26
  Tugenhaft (grocers), 26
Johnston, Ebenezer Forsyth
  Blackie, 73, 74, 77, 86, 90-92,
    98-100, 102-105, 107, 111, 113,
    114, 122-124, 127, 132-137, 139,
    143, 144, 149, 150, 154, 155, 157,
    158
Jurors, jury, 7, 15, 34, 65, 71, 73,
  76-84, 92, 96-98, 102, 104, 105,
  108, 112-114, 120, 124, 127, 132-
  138, 140-151, 153

Kennedy, Warring (Mayor), 137
Knowles, James, 65, 66
Kraft-Ebing, Richard von (Dr.), 58

Lake Ontario, 1, 4, 6, 8, 11, 14,
  106, 159
Lakeside Hall (Parkdale), 1, 2, 6,
  11, 12, 41, 64, 68, 84, 101, 159
Lennox, Ed, 14, 25, 89
Lepovsky and Berman, see Jewish
  shops
Liberals (provincial), 152
Lombroso, Cesare, 150
Low, David, 12, 97, 102
Lynd, Adam (Dr.), 3, 9, 10, 37

Macaulaytown (St. John's Ward),
  46
Macdonald, John A. (Sir), 23, 73
MacMahon, Hugh (Justice), 77
Mail, see Toronto newspapers
Male sexual fantasies, 158

Manitoba, Province of, 48

Manning, Maria, 82

Markham (ON), 143

Massey, ___ (Mrs.), 151

Massey, Charles, 151

McKay, (Florence) Flora, 25, 26, 28, 29, 31, 38, 39, 41, 48-50, 52, 62, 63, 72, 87, 89-91, 98, 101, 117, 123, 136, 137, 142, 146

McKay, Jessie (Mrs.), 37, 45, 49, 50

McLaughlin, James, 131

McMaster University, 79

M'Naghton case (1843), 60

Meldum, William, 131

Mitchell, Alice, 61

Moore's Musée, 23, 156

Morgentaler case, 151

Mount Pleasant Cemetery (Toronto), 8

Murdoch, William G., 35-37, 39-41, 72-74, 76, 77, 85, 88, 90, 91, 95, 112, 113, 115, 122, 132, 137, 139, 144

Murphy, ___ (lawyer), 35

Murphy, Mary, 94

New Fort (Toronto), 31, 69, 101, 103, 127

New York (NY), 66, 67

Newmarket (ON), 143

News, see Toronto newspapers

Niagara Falls, 66

Northwest Rebellion (1885), 24, 49

Oakley, George, 113

Observer (Sarnia), 42

Of Toronto the Good: A Social Study: The Queen City of Canada As It Is, 18

Old Fort (Toronto), 103

Ontario Provincial Police, 154

Opera House (Toronto), 10, 23, 25, 26, 104, 117-119, 123, 131

Orange-Green Riots, 20

Orange Lodge (provincial), 153

Orr, R.B. (Dr.) (Coroner), 8, 13, 15, 86

Osgoodby Building (Toronto), 75, 76

Osgoode Hall (Toronto), 26

Osler:

    Britton Bath (B.B.) (Crown prosecutor), 79-86, 90, 92, 93, 98, 100, 107, 108, 132, 149

        background of, 79

    Carrie, 108

    Edmund, 79

    Featherstone, 79

    William (Dr.), 79

Owen Sound (ON), 46

Oxford County, 31

Palmer, ___ (Mrs.), 51

Palmer House (Toronto), 51

Park Street Public School, 45

Parkdale, town of, see Toronto

Parkdale Methodist Church, 4, 7

Peel, Robert (British Prime Minister), 60

Peer, Albert, 9

Phyle, ___ (Mrs.), 89-91

Phyle family, 50

Police Court, 20, 35, 37, 47, 103

Police Stations (Toronto):

    No. 6, 3

    Queen Street division, 13

Pollock, Joseph, 143

Porter, George (Detective), 5, 25-27, 40, 42, 91, 116, 128, 134, 138

Presbyterian, 45

Princeton (ON), 81
Prostitution, prostitutes, 17, 27, 36, 48, 80
Protestants, 20, 25
Psychopathia Sexualis, 58

Quebec, Province of, 45, 60, 69
Queen's Park (Toronto), 23

Rabinowich, see Jewish shops
Race, racial background, 31, 35, 38, 40, 45, 70, 72, 94, 121
Randolph, John, 94
Rape, 70
Reburn, Henry (Sergeant of Detectives), 27-32, 34-36, 40-42, 63, 64, 67, 69, 90, 97-103, 116-119, 121, 127, 131, 134, 153, 154
Reid, Eliza, 131, 143, 146
Riel, Louis, 79, 162
Robinette, T.C., 154
Rochester (NY), 48
Rogers, Nicholas, 20
Role of women, 70, 71
Roman Catholics, Catholics, 20
Royal Grenadiers (Toronto), 24
Russell, H.M., 36

Sadism, 60
Salvation Army Industrial Home for Young Women, 11, 25, 49
Sam T. Jack's Creoles, 158
Sarnia (ON), 42
Scandal in Bohemia, A, 55
Schiller Hotel (Toronto), 96
Scott, E.F. (Rev.), 4, 6, 7
Sentinel (Orange Lodge), 153
"Sherlock Holmes," see Doyle, Arthur Conan
Sherwood, Samuel, 10, 21

Simpson's Department Store, 117
Slemin, Charles (Detective), 4, 13, 14, 25-27, 40, 42, 63, 1, 116, 118, 128, 131, 134, 19, 154
Sparrow, ___ (Dr.), 3
Spectator (Hamilton), 108, 150
St. Luke's Anglican Church (Toronto), 45
Star, see Toronto newspapers
Stark, William (Inspector) (Chief of Detectives), 4, 5, 18, 27, 28, 32, 40, 41, 65, 104, 105, 116, 117, 122, 123, 131, 134, 154
Steinberg, Vic, 56, 75, 117
Stephen, Bessie, 10
Stow, ___ (Mrs.), 44, 45
Strange, Carolyn, 70, 123
Stratford (ON), 60
Street, William (Justice), 76, 77
Sturgeon, Lizzie (Miss), 23
Syracuse (NY), 48

Tavern, licensed, 17
Telegram, see Toronto newspapers
Temperance League Coffee House (Toronto), 39
Tennessee, 61
Thompson, W.J., 127
Toronto (Queen City) (ON), ii, iii, 1, 4-6, 16-18, 20-24, 26, 33, 35, 36, 44, 46, 47, 50, 54, 58, 65, 69, 71, 75, 78, 80, 93, 107, 113, 115, 117, 126, 146, 150, 151, 159
    attitudes toward Blacks, 31, 46-48, 72, 94
    bylaws, 17, 18
    description of in 1890s, 16, 17, 20-23
    industrial activity, 21, 22
    streetcars, 20, 21, 23

Toronto City Council, 47
Toronto districts:
 Parkdale, 1, 8, 16, 22, 26, 29-31,
 38, 39, 41, 49, 51, 56, 58, 63, 89,
 90, 93, 104, 116, 142, 159
 St. John's Ward (the Ward), 26,
 27, 46, 94, 159
Toronto newspapers:
 Empire, 11, 30, 40, 112
 Globe, 14, 17, 21, 32, 33, 35, 41,
 42, 44, 75, 77, 89, 105, 122, 124,
 126, 141, 144, 152, 153, 159
 Mail, 4, 11, 42, 51, 52, 56
 News, 7-9, 12, 13, 36, 38, 56, 59,
 64, 65, 75, 76, 78, 86, 88, 95,
 96, 102, 120, 126, 128, 135, 145,
 150, 152-154
 Star, 32, 67, 140, 144, 147, 151-
 153
 Telegram, 14, 41, 48, 55, 58, 65,
 67-70, 74, 92, 105, 110, 124, 126,
 127, 132, 140, 142, 147
 World, 5, 10, 15, 17, 20, 21, 33,
 35, 44, 49, 55, 58, 59, 72, 84, 94,
 109, 113, 117, 119, 124, 126, 127,
 142, 148, 149, 153, 156, 157
Toronto Police Force, 5, 6, 18-20,
 25, 42, 43, 51, 60, 61, 70, 137,
 152-154
 background of, 18, 25
 Department of Detectives, 18
 public perception of, 20
Toronto streets:
 Adelaide Street, 77, 95, 139
 Bathurst Street, 68, 69
 Bay Street, 89, 117
 Bloor Street, 159
 Camden Street, 41, 87, 119
 College Street, 54
 Dominion Street, 30, 68, 101

Dufferin Street, 30, 41, 68, 69
Gloucester Street, 45
Jameson Avenue, 2-4, 7, 10, 30,
 41, 68, 159
Jarvis Street, 25
King Street, 10, 16, 21, 93
Massey Street, 93
Melinda Street, 75
Queen Street, 26, 50, 89, 117
Richmond Street, 117
Spencer Avenue, 93
Yonge Street, 10, 26, 75, 117, 143
York Street, 25, 26, 50, 116, 128,
 131, 156
Transvestite, 60
Treatise on Domestic Economy, 70
Trinity United Church (Toronto),
 159
Tugenhaft, see Jewish shops

Union Station (Toronto), 154
United States, 20, 22, 46-48, 51,
 73, 81, 94
 attitudes toward Blacks, 46, 94

Veblen, Thurstein, 54
Victorian fashion (women), 53-55
Vise, Benjamin, 51, 109, 110

Ward, Freda, 61
Ward (St. John's Ward), see
 Toronto districts
Welter, Barbara, 70
Westwood:
 Benjamin, 2, 3, 8-10, 22, 25, 38,
 85, 86, 97, 102, 139, 140, 144,
 147, 158
 Clara (Mrs. B.), 1-3, 22, 37, 85,
 147, 159
 Frank B., 1-16, 27, 28, 30-33, 36,

37, 39, 40, 50, 58-61, 64, 68,
70, 83-88, 90-93, 95, 101, 102,
104, 106-108, 112, 116, 118, 121,
124, 133, 140, 142, 146, 148, 151,
156, 159
  shooting of, 1, 2
  Herbert, 50
  William "Willie," 2, 3
Whitechapel murders, 80
Windsor (ON), 46
Winks, Robin, 47
Women:
  attitudes toward, 70, 71
  chivalry, 149-151
  salaries, 17, 71
  work in Toronto, 71
Woodstock (ON), 81
Workman, Elizabeth, 42
World (Toronto), see Toronto
  newspapers

York County, 70, 96

Patrick Brode was born in Windsor, Ontario. He was called to the Ontario Bar in 1977 and has practised law ever since. He has written four works on the history of law in Canada including *Sir John Beverley Robinson: Bone and Sinew of the Compact*, a finalist for the City of Toronto Book Award in 1985, and *The Odyssey of John Anderson*, a finalist for the Trillium Award in 1990.